Diamond Diva

First published in Great Britain in 2008 by

André Deutsch
an imprint of the
Carlton Publishing Group
20 Mortimer Street
London W1T 3JW

2 4 6 8 10 9 7 5 3 1

The publishers would like to thank the following sources for their kind
permission to reproduce the pictures in this book.

Page 1: Mirrorpix
Page 2: (top) William Lovelace/Express/Getty Images; (bottom) Peter Hall/
Keystone Features/Getty Images
Page 3: (top) PA Photos; (bottom) Everett Collection/Rex Features
Page 4: (top) R. McPhedran/Express/Getty Images; (bottom) Evening
Standard/Hulton Archive/Getty Images
Page 5: (top) Powell/Express/Getty Images; (bottom) Harry Myers/Rex Features
Page 6: (top) PA Photos; (bottom) Topfoto.co.uk
Page 7: (top) Rex Features; (bottom) Nils Jorgensen/Rex Features
Page 8: (top) Yui Mok/PA Photos; (bottom) Leon Schadeberg/Rex Features

Every effort has been made to acknowledge correctly and contact the
source and/or copyright holder of each picture and Carlton Books
Limited apologises for any unintentional errors or omissions, which
will be corrected in future editions of this book..

A catalogue record for this book is available from the British Library

ISBN 978-0-233-00238-5

Typeset by E-Type, Liverpool
Printed and bound in Great Britain by Mackays

SHIRLEY
BASSEY

Diamond Diva

PETER HOGAN

André Deutsch

For Debbie Geller, who knew how to laugh.

Contents

Acknowledgements

For this book I've drawn upon articles and interviews with Dame Shirley Bassey from numerous newspaper and magazine sources, including the *Sunday Times*, the *Independent*, the *Daily Mail*, the *Telegraph*, *Ebony*, the *Sunday Mirror*, the *Guardian*, the *South Wales Echo*, the *People*, the *Miami New Times*, *After Dark*, *FHM*, *Saga*, *OK!*, *Hello*, *Privé*, *Gay Times*, *New Idea*, *My Weekly* and *Picture Show*.

I've also relied upon a number of books, especially Dame Shirley Bassey's own *My Life On Record And In Concert* (Bloomsbury Publishing, 1998), Garth Bardsley's *Stop The World : The Biography of Anthony Newley* (Oberon Books, 2003), *Feminine Power* by Mona Bauwens and Peter Thompson (Mainstream Publishing, 1998), *Shirley* by Muriel Burgess (Arrow Books, 1999), *Stars In My Eyes* by Max Bygraves (Robson Books, 2003), *A Touch Of Collins* by Joe Collins (Headline, 1987), Joan Collins' *My Friends' Secrets* (André Deutsch, 1999), Elaine Dundy's *Finch, Bloody Finch* (Holt, Rinehart And Winston, 1980), Trader Faulkner's *Peter Finch* (Angus & Robertson, 1979), Eddi Fiegel's *John Barry : A Sixties Theme* (Constable, 1998), Graham McCann's *Morecambe & Wise* (Fourth Estate, 1998), Michael Sullivan's *There's No People Like Show People: Confessions Of A Showbiz Agent* (Quadrant Books, 1984) and Carey Wallace's interview with Dame Shirley and Douglas Darnell in the catalogue for Christie's Gala Charity

Auction *Dame Shirley Bassey: 50 Years Of Glittering Gowns* (Christie's, 2003). I'm also indebted to all the fan websites dedicated to Dame Shirley, and to all the Bassey fans (you know who you are) who offered helpful advice and information.

My thanks to Dieter Meier of Yello and Nick Robinson, who granted me interviews, and the Butetown History & Arts Centre, for answering all my questions about Cardiff in the 1930s. Thanks also to Steve Davis at EMI, Peter at Dieter Meier's office and Hik Sasaki at WEA for making connections; and to John Knowles and Paul Carey, for trying anyway.

On a personal level I'm indebted to Patrick Humphries for the heads up; to my wife Ellie, Ruth Hogan and Maureen Hughes for manning the home front; to Vanessa Morgan for the hospitality; to Penny Phillips of André Deutsch for commissioning me to write this book in the first place; to Lara Maiklem, who gamely held the fort; and finally, a special thanks to my editor Rod Green, for his patience and much more besides.

Peter Hogan, London 2008

OF DIAMONDS
AND DIVAS

At the 2007 Glastonbury Festival, just five months after celebrating her seventieth birthday, Dame Shirley Bassey strode onto the open-air Pyramid stage at 5.20 on the Sunday afternoon, wearing a pink Julien MacDonald dress that was slit to the thigh. Accompanied by a full orchestra (with conductor), she then performed a 45-minute selection of her greatest hits to an ecstatic, enraptured audience – most of whom were probably not even born when Dame Shirley began her musical career. For many of them the inclusion of 'Light My Fire' in her set alongside 'Goldfinger' and 'Big Spender' probably came as a bit of a shock, but the truth was that she'd recorded her own version of the Doors' song nearly 40 years earlier (and the line 'no time to wallow in the mire' certainly seemed appropriate for a crowd struggling in the Glastonbury mud, which was several feet deep in places that year). Two nights earlier at the Festival, the Arctic Monkeys had included a version of 'Diamonds Are Forever' in their set; after performing the song herself, Dame Shirley quipped, 'Arctic Monkeys, that's how it's done', and the crowd roared its approval.

'It turned into a great big singalong,' promoter Harvey Goldsmith later commented of her performance. 'She went out and slayed 'em.' Watching Dame Shirley from the wings had been another artist who had also made his Glastonbury debut that year: Pete Townshend, guitarist of The Who, who later proudly declared, 'I have always been a fan.' In his Internet blog Townshend commented: 'Watching DSB I was reminded what makes a performer matter, what makes them last, what makes them great. Humility, humour and love. DSB still has a great voice (and I can assure you the conditions at Glasto were awful for her and her orchestra on stage as well as off). She is still very, very sexy. She triumphed at Glastonbury.' One of those who agreed with the verdicts of Goldsmith and Townshend was Michael Eavis, the Festival's organizer, who described Dame Shirley's appearance as being 'one of the highlights of the weekend. The sun certainly shone for Dame Shirley when she took to that stage'; another was the music critic Peter Paphides, whose review of the Festival in *The Times* singled out only two of the acts for special mention, these being the modern-day British songstress Lily Allen and Dame Shirley Bassey. She herself later admitted that she'd been 'extremely nervous. It certainly wasn't my normal crowd. But I ended up really enjoying it. I found it exhilarating, getting this chance to do that. I love doing different things.'

After the Festival was over, on its way back to her hotel in Bagshot, Dame Shirley's helicopter developed problems due to bad weather and the pilot was forced to make an emergency landing in the playing fields of Collingwood College in Camberley, Surrey. The school caretaker had to let Dame Shirley out of the locked grounds, and although unhurt she was said to have been shaken by her experience (although she later denied that she'd even been worried: 'We were laughing and joking. We knew we were in safe hands.'). Dame Shirley spent several minutes chatting with the small crowd of people that the helicopter landing had attracted, and even posed for photos with them; she also happily accepted the hospitality of one local resident, who allowed her to use his toilet. 'I could hear his wife on the phone while I was in there, telling people about her unexpected visitor,' she later revealed. All of this was captured by eager news cameras, which took delight in focusing on Dame Shirley's green wellington boots. These bore the initials 'DSB' spelled out in diamanté 'gems' – the boots having been customized by the nine-year-old daughter of one of her friends. They had been an essential part of Dame Shirley's Glastonbury wardrobe, since the mud level backstage was just as bad as it was for the audience. Some press reports had suggested that the 'gems' might actually be diamonds – and the truth is, no one would have been really surprised if they had been.

*

Dame Shirley Bassey was born only two years after Elvis Presley and a mere three years before John Lennon, but rock 'n' roll itself had barely been invented when she first took to the stage (and both Presley and Lennon were still at school at the time). Even disc jockeys and pop charts were still very recent developments then – and Shirley's main rivals in those charts were not to be Elvis or the Beatles, or even Tommy Steele or Cliff Richard. Initially, her main competition came from the orthodox showbiz world of Vera Lynn and Liberace and the Beverley Sisters (as well as acts too ghastly for musical history to even remember, like Pearl Carr and Teddy Johnson, Dickie Valentine and Miki & Griff). She was a part of the orthodox showbiz world herself; in those days, that was the only kind of showbiz there was.

Most young people have no real idea what the 1950s (or even the 1960s and 1970s) were actually like in Britain, because they believe the clichés. The reality was a much bleaker and greyer world than they could imagine, punctuated only by the occasional flash of colour ... And Shirley Bassey was undeniably one of those flashes. In the 1950s Britain was suffering through the era of post-war austerity, with food rationing still in place; for most people, apart from a weekly visit to the cinema, entertainment was still largely a live experience, and – serious theatre aside – consisted mainly of variety shows and revues. Until 1955 there was only one television channel in operation, and although many people undoubtedly bought TV sets to watch the coronation of Queen Elizabeth II, they remained very much in the minority until ITV came on the air two years later. Then, TV became a phenomenon that exploded so quickly that it was widely regarded, in the words of Lew Grade, as 'a licence to print money.' It coincided with the early days of Miss Bassey's career, and she took full advantage of it; her first record deal even came about simply because a producer caught her act on a late-night TV music show.

In those days popular music was very definitely thought of by almost everybody as being merely 'light entertainment'; the aspirations towards it becoming an artform would only follow a decade later, in the wake of the Beatles and Bob Dylan. Singers in the

1950s were still just a part of 'show business', a loose term which also embraced comedians, acrobats, ventriloquists, conjurors and animal acts – and the business itself was totally dominated and controlled by a small handful of impresarios like Jack Hylton, Val Parnell, and Lew and Leslie Grade, who worked in conjunction with booking agents, managers and music publishers. It was a system that had remained virtually unchanged since the days of music hall. Singers then also simply did not, as a rule, write their own songs (something else which only really changed with the emergence of the Beatles); placing songs with singers was almost entirely the province of the music publishers of Tin Pan Alley, otherwise known as London's Denmark Street.

But although Shirley Bassey largely conformed to many of the traditions of the business, she was also able to blast her way through all the cosy 'How Much Is That Doggie' status quo with a barrage of sheer sex appeal, of which her wicked sense of humour was as much a key ingredient as her shimmering, skintight costumes or her seductive hand gestures. After all, she's had to put up with the 'burley chassis' nickname for most of her career, and her collaboration with Morecambe and Wise alone proves she's as much a comedienne as a femme fatale.

Certainly, there had been nothing quite like her before in Britain, or anywhere else for that matter. Even Eartha Kitt's feline come-ons seemed quietly restrained by comparison. The poet Philip Larkin once famously observed that sexual intercourse began in 1963 – an exaggeration, but it's undeniably true that that was the era when it came out into the open as a subject, largely thanks to the Profumo affair and the *Lady Chatterley* trial; prior to those events, sex was barely ever discussed in public. Admittedly, there were still sex symbols of the day – mainly actresses like Bardot and Monroe, or Britain's own Diana Dors and Joan Collins, but Shirley Bassey was one of the few singers of the era who joined their ranks. The reason was simple: she positively radiated sexuality; she always had done, and she always would.

*

Speaking of sex and the Sixties, it's significant that Dame Shirley managed to weld her career to the sexiest movie franchise of the decade (and indeed, the late twentieth century). The only artist to record more than one James Bond theme (she racked up three), Dame Shirley is so linked to 007 in the public imagination that a few years ago market research discovered that people questioned in the street were unable to name any other singer besides her who'd recorded a Bond theme. 'The world is ready for another Shirley Bassey Bond theme,' claimed music producer David Arnold in 1997; he wanted her to sing the title theme for that year's Bond film, *Tomorrow Never Dies*, but in the end he was outvoted by the marketing men. Still, the perceived connection persists, something that the Marks & Spencer chain were able to trade upon for their Christmas 2006 advertising campaign; when the cabaret act in the Bond-inspired ice palace is revealed to be DSB performing her distinctive cover version of Pink's 'Get The Party Started', it's a moment of camp perfection.

*

But the sex appeal was just the icing on the cake. Her biggest asset, of course, was the fact that she was (and is) possessed of a real powerhouse of a voice, which early on earned her the nickname of 'Bassey The Belter.' 'I've always attacked a song,' she once admitted, although she also confessed that the 'Belter' nickname had upset her at the time. Yet her voice seems utterly effortless, despite its power. There are many in recent years who have compared Dame Shirley's style and approach to that of opera singers; the journalist Simon Fanshawe even recently described her as being 'half tomboy, half Maria Callas.' Dame Shirley herself was delighted when the American soprano Jessye Norman told her that she [Norman] couldn't sing like that herself; Norman's performances consisted of short bursts scattered through the length of an entire opera, which required a lot less endurance than singing song after song for a period of an hour and a half, as Dame Shirley did.

Those songs are carefully selected, and she's always had a good ear for new material; it's something which has shaped both her recordings and her live performances. She has described the process of selecting songs for her stage act as being 'like writing a story.' The perfect opening song is required, and the perfect closing number, and then everything in between needs to be placed in the perfect order, which often requires rejigging; a great song may fall flat when placed in one part of the sequence, but triumph if moved to an earlier or later slot. As a whole, the songs complement each other and tell a larger story – whether torch songs or power ballads, they speak of love and loss and betrayal, of survival and self-respect.

'You have to sing songs that the audience can identify with,' Dame Shirley has observed in the past. In the early years of her career this meant relying on standards, that were familiar to the audience through other people's versions; as time went on, she endeavoured to replace these with songs that were either written specifically for her or which she had personally discovered. Either way, they had to strike a personal chord with her: 'It's so important to believe in a song, because when you do, then you can sell it to the audience and they will believe in it too.' She has also obviously always felt a real passion for what she was singing, and once commented, 'Everything I sing on that stage is me.'

In live performances she'd usually stand rooted to the spot, frequently making dramatic, emotional gestures with her hands and body: the hands extended and pushing outwards, as if holding bad news at bay; or caressing the front of her body, her hand clutching at her heart; or else her outstretched arms are flung wide, as if offering to embrace the entire audience. 'Sometimes I'm not even aware of those movements, because I'm so carried away. Not every night, though. That depends on the audience.' At every show in recent years, her fans approach the stage to give her lavishly wrapped gifts, or to shake her hand; a lucky few get a kiss. (In the past, people have been known to squeeze Dame Shirley's hands so tightly that her rings cut into her fingers until they bled. Now, she removes them before each performance).

While singing her eyes flash, she grins and snarls, whispers and shouts; she not only catches the audience's eye, but actively flirts with them. On several occasions she's chosen to refer to herself as 'a performer' rather than a singer, and it's an interesting distinction; she's at least in part an actress, truly larger-than-life both on stage and off.

And those spectacular costumes of hers have always been a vital part of the performance. Viewers in the 1970s were known to tune in to Shirley's TV show *just* in order to see what she was wearing this time, and her gowns were masterpieces of engineering: often backless, strapless or sideless (and sometimes all three), they added an element of suspense to the proceedings, as audiences wondered if this might be the night when she'd bust through the sequins completely. On at least one occasion it actually happened, as she recalled in 2000: 'All of those old costumes were treacherous. In the early days I was taking my body into my hands every time I performed! Whenever I heaved my bosom to take in a breath for a top note . . . oh, God! But I learned to live with it and not worry about things going wrong – and then one day the dreaded thing did happen. The gown split and started to fall, and I grabbed my breast – but it looked like I was grabbing my chest and everyone thought I was having a heart attack. And the song, believe it or not, was "The Lady is a Tramp".' This number, originally from the Rodgers and Hart musical *Pal Joey*, is a song that Dame Shirley has totally reworked, not only by fusing it into a medley with 'He's a Tramp' (Peggy Lee's blues from Disney's *Lady and the Tramp*), but also by performing it as a first-person statement of defiance. This is what I am, she tells the listener; take it or leave it.

All of this has endeared her to a gay following as well as a straight one, and from early on in her career she became an icon for drag queens, something which she took in her stride. 'I can see them in the audience, which gives me power to give more. I can actually see them – that's why I have lights on the audience, so I can see them. There's no point in being a singer if you can't see audience reaction. They identify with the songs I sing. They're about love lost, love won. "I Am What I Am", which they call the gay anthem, and

"This Is My Life." They identify with that: even if I'm gay and everybody is against me it doesn't matter. This is my life and I am what I am.' On another occasion, she aired her feeling that her emotional appeal was not only a musical one, but also personal: 'My gay fans have always liked the roller-coaster of my life. You know: she's gone through all this and she's still up there.'

*

As for Dame Shirley's own life: hers may seem a fairly straightforward rags-to-riches story, the poor girl who made good in the end. Superficially, it seems like a show business cliché – but that view doesn't really take into account just how high the walls that she had to climb actually were. To be a poor factory girl from a mixed-race background in the 1950s was a combination of what were then three almost insurmountable obstacles to success: poverty, class and race. Added to this was the fact that Shirley was the teenage mother of an illegitimate child, which was totally beyond the pale in those days, to the point of causing complete moral outrage. Yet she overcame all of these obstacles, becoming an established star within the space of only a few years; in the process she transformed herself into the Shirley Bassey we all know. Fifty years after she began her career, she has become both an icon and a diva. The drive and determination it must have taken to accomplish this are both impressive and admirable.

After becoming a star her story becomes a mixture of mystery and melodrama, with the heroine enduring failed marriages, death and disaster en route to a kind of mythic isolation, the goddess alone with her Voice. She's had self-knowledge enough to concede that she's made more than her share of romantic mistakes in her time, perhaps best expressed in her choosing to perform the song 'Nobody Does It Like Me' in concert. Written by Cy Coleman and Dorothy Fields (who also wrote 'Big Spender'), the lyric runs: 'If there's a wrong way to do it, a right way to screw it up, nobody does it like me.' However, tales of romantic disaster are ones that we can all relate to, for most have us have had our hearts broken and most us have survived – but Dame Shirley has lived through at least one genuine tragedy that no one should have to endure, because no parent should have to outlive their own child.

*

Against all the odds, she's still in business. Very few 'easy listening' acts of the 1960s and 1970s have managed to cross over into mass acceptance by a modern audience – Burt Bacharach and Frank Sinatra spring to mind, and there are perhaps a handful of others, Dame Shirley Bassey among them. If the parade of her hits slowed down after her 1960s and 1970s heyday, it never stopped entirely; in the 50 years between 1957 and 2007, Dame Shirley Bassey racked up no less than 32 hit singles, and 35 hit albums. Not only is this a record in itself, it also officially makes her the most successful female British recording artist of all time. Like very few other singers (such as Johnny Cash, and Frank Sinatra once again), Dame Shirley looks set to continue performing for as long as she is able. In a recent poll, she was named as one of the 100 most famous people of the twentieth century.

*

Over the years, Dame Shirley Bassey has had good reason to distrust the press – especially the tabloid press. 'What they didn't know, they made up,' she once complained. As a result, she grants few interviews and seems completely unconcerned about courting the media; she does not need the fees offered by the press, or at least not for herself – she donated the fee from a recent *Daily Mail* interview to the War Widows Association. And when she does talk to the press, she's renowned for refusing to answer questions about her personal life; the lady has come to guard her privacy carefully. This is at least partly the reason why she has 'never written my own material. I don't even write poetry or keep a diary. I will never put down anything intimate again, even in love letters. Because it can be used against you.'

When I began writing this book I naturally approached Dame Shirley's office, in the hope that she might grant me an interview, or co-operate with this book in some other way. I received no replies to my inquiries, but I subsequently stumbled across this quote from a 1993 interview that Dame Shirley gave to *OK!* magazine's Martin Smith, which goes some way to explaining why I never heard back from her: 'I wouldn't have my life made into a film. I wouldn't even write a book. I've been asked many times, but I don't believe in it. It seems that the moment somebody becomes famous they must write and tell all, but I am not a kiss-and-tell person. I am quite a private person. Somebody wrote an unauthorized book and I read the first page and closed it and never picked it up again. It was a load of rubbish. I've never met the person who wrote it and I don't want to.'

After reading the pages that follow, Dame Shirley may well feel the same way about this book and this author, but I hope not. For what it's worth, in the course of researching this book I heard a good deal of scurrilous gossip about Dame Shirley's youth, and as far as I can tell, absolutely none of it was true, or even contained a *grain* of truth. I've also done my best to avoid repeating obviously unfounded rumours from earlier accounts, and was surprised at just how often the same inaccurate information has been presented as fact in newspaper articles down the years. Even so, if Dame Shirley truly feels that some aspects of her reported life are 'a load of rubbish', it seems a shame that she has declined this opportunity to set the record straight – although I sympathize deeply with her feelings on this matter, and her desire to be left alone. Regardless, I've attempted to separate fact from fiction here, and to deliver a balanced assessment of Dame Shirley's life and work; hopefully both she and her fans will feel that I've done her justice as an artist and as a person.

In the end, what can one say about Dame Shirley Bassey? She is without doubt an extremely complex person: talented, driven, vulnerable, tireless, humorous, prickly, flamboyant, private, demanding, giving . . . in short, a diva.

And a diamond one, at that.

One

THE TIGER CUB

The city of Cardiff has been a trading port since Roman times. Situated on the Bristol Channel at the mouth of the River Taff, by the early years of the twentieth century the Welsh capital had become the largest coal-exporting port in the world, with ships from all over the world docking there to load up their holds with the produce from Welsh mines. The waterway leading to the harbour acquired the memorable nickname of Tiger Bay early in the early nineteenth century, supposedly as a result of a Portuguese sailor claiming that the waters were so dangerous to navigate that it was like sailing through a bay of tigers. The name was subsequently used to refer to the whole area surrounding the docklands, but in the 1960s Cardiff council officially named this area Cardiff Bay, although many locals still refer to it as simply 'The Bay.' The name change was presumably an attempt to put an end to the area's reputation for notoriety of all kinds. For Tiger Bay was not only once a working-class slum; it was also, in the words of Shirley Bassey's first manager Michael Sullivan, 'one of the roughest, toughest parts of Britain.'

Today, Cardiff is the fastest-growing city in the UK, with

numerous brand-new office blocks and a futuristic sports stadium rubbing shoulders with the medieval castle and the Victorian shopping arcades. Running from the city centre down to the Bay is Bute Street, named after the aristocratic Bute family who once owned Cardiff Castle and did much to generally improve the city in the nineteenth century. Many of the other streets in the Bay were named after the Earl of Bute's numerous daughters, and an alternative name for Tiger Bay – which still remains in use – is 'Butetown.' A few hundred yards away from the end of Bute Street on the waterfront itself is a structure which explains the Bute family's interest in the area: a large and impressive redbrick Victorian building, reminiscent of a medieval castle, which was once the headquarters of the Bute Docks Company. Outside the building two ancient cannon stand pointing out at the water; presumably these were once a vital part of the harbour's defence system in the event of a foreign invasion.

But today small craft no longer ferry imported produce across the Bay to Barry Island, and the docks and their slag heaps have long since vanished. The waterfront and its environs is now dominated by brand-new art galleries, gift boutiques and restaurants; a few hundred yards from the Bute Docks building stands the Wales Millennium Centre, which in recent years has become a familiar sight to all viewers of *Dr Who*. Only a few streets near the harbour date back to the nineteenth century; the vast majority of the area – including the Bute Street birthplace of Shirley Bassey – was bulldozed in the late 1950s, to make way for tower blocks and a low-rise council estate. Still, the area's history and multi-cultural heritage clearly remains important to its inhabitants, and the course of upper Bute Street is punctuated with engraved steel bollards that mark the former sites of local landmarks: the Caribbean Club, the Somali Boarding House, the Wah Lee Chinese Laundry. Engraved slabs in the pavement contain the names of noted former residents of the area, including that of Dame Shirley Bassey.

A glimpse of the area as it once was can be found in the 1959 British thriller *Tiger Bay*, which was actually shot on location in the area. Both the film and a behind-the-scenes documentary on its filming show Tiger Bay as consisting mainly of run-down and dilapidated tenement buildings, with a population that was visibly far more multi-racial than most of Britain at the time. And it had been that way for a long time. Tiger Bay even suffered its first race riot as far back as 1919, when the area barricaded itself against an invasion by white Welshmen on horseback, who were protesting because immigrant black men were 'taking their jobs'; the residents defended themselves so fiercely during scuffles at the barricades that not one of the protesters succeeded in entering the area. By the 1930s the population of Tiger Bay included not only black Africans, but also North Africans and Arabs, Chinese, Serbs, Greeks and Europeans of all kinds, as well as its original Welsh inhabitants. There was a halal butcher's, a Chinese laundry, and many other businesses which would have been deemed 'exotic' in the rest of Britain, while West Indian men played dice games on the street corners and the area boasted a disproportionately large number of pubs and clubs and dancehalls. Like many harbour areas Tiger Bay was also a red-light district, with the number of brothels rapidly growing during the Second World

War because of the number of British and American servicemen stationed in the town. Supposedly, local children at the time were delighted that the glamorous young 'aunties' they'd see on the streets would pass on to them the sweets they'd been given by their sailor customers.

*

This was the world that surrounded Shirley Veronica Bassey when she was born on 8 January 1937, at the family residence of 182 Bute Street (she shares her birthday with both Elvis Presley and David Bowie). Shirley's father, Henry Bassey, was a Nigerian merchant seaman – a ship's fireman, to be specific – who had settled in Cardiff in the 1920s; according to Shirley's biographer Muriel Burgess, Henry originally came from Calobar, and was a member of the Efik tribe. Shirley's mother Eliza Jane (formerly Metcalfe) came from either Yorkshire or North Shields on the Tyne (accounts vary).

The Basseys already had six children when Shirley was born: Gracie, Ella, Iris, twins Eileen and Henry, and Marina. Shirley was a popular girl's name at the time, probably because Shirley Temple was then one of the biggest stars in Hollywood, but Burgess claims that Henry always called his youngest daughter by the nickname of 'Sharon', which had supposedly been a pet name for the Queen of Sheba. If true, this would explain Shirley's eventual choice of that name for her own daughter. The Bassey home was a smallish two-storey house, at one end of a terraced street, and so crowded that the children slept three to a bed; according to Burgess the family income was sometimes supplemented by sub-letting a room to sailors, and the house became even more crowded at weekends, because Henry was keen on holding impromptu parties.

Shirley would retain fond childhood memories of her mother, as she told the *Independent*'s Deborah Ross: 'She was quite Victorian in many ways. She was a quiet Northern woman with beautiful, very white, skin, who didn't give much away about herself and was a great cook. I remember her egg and bacon tarts. And her Yorkshire puddings. We also had a lot of offal, because offal was cheap, but I hated it.' Shirley and her mother would always be close, but her father was another matter.

Henry left the Bassey home for good when Shirley was between two and three years old, and in interviews she's never given any further explanation for his departure. Muriel Burgess claims that Henry was an illegal immigrant who'd effectively jumped ship in Cardiff, and had never legalized his residency in Britain; she also states that the reason for his sudden departure was because the authorities finally caught up with him, and deported him back to Nigeria. Whatever the reasons, Shirley never saw her father again, nor does she have any personal recollection of him, although her mother is said to have told her often that her father was 'a good man and he always loved you.' Shirley once recalled that, 'My sister Marina, who's two years older than me, used to write to him and she'd tell me stories. But all I've got is one photo to remember him by.' Asked in the 1990s about her Nigerian roots, Shirley replied that she'd 'never had any great desire to go there', and she revealed to Deborah Ross that as far as her father went, 'I never even asked my mother about him. I didn't want to carry that baggage through my life. I just let it go.' Doubtless Henry's departure was a deeply traumatic event for his young daughter, and perhaps she has never forgiven him for it.

But Henry may still have had a profoundly positive influence upon at least one aspect of Shirley's life. Her mother once commented that she thought Shirley 'got her singing from her father. He was always so fond of music. He never stopped playing gramophone records. Shirley used to sing with them as a tiny girl.' Unlikely as this may seem, given how young Shirley was when her father left, her sister Gracie once confirmed that Shirley 'sang as soon as she could talk. The neighbours liked to listen to her.' Even Shirley has admitted that she has no explanation for the origins of her voice: 'Nobody in my family sings, nobody from my mother's side. We don't know about my father's side. There was probably some ancestor out there chanting for rain with this powerful voice centuries ago.' But music was impossible to avoid in Tiger Bay, for it was just as important to the immigrant communities as it was, traditionally, to the Welsh. It spilled out into the streets from local pubs like the Ship and Pilot, from the constant neighbourhood parties, from the Saturday-night dances at the Annexe Hall and the 'threepenny hops' at the Old Vestry.

The Bassey family moved away from Tiger Bay in 1940, when Shirley was three years old. This may have been providential for them, since Cardiff was badly bombed three times a few months later, during March 1941. The docks were naturally one of the Luftwaffe's prime targets (and would again be the target for V1 'doodlebugs' later in the war), but fortunately at least some of the bombs landed harmlessly in the mud of the Bay. At least three houses in Butetown were less lucky, and were totally destroyed. Local historians think the Nazis may have also been trying to destroy the factory of Curran's Engineering Works – where Shirley would eventually work, after leaving school – since during the 1940s the firm was engaged on munitions work for the war effort, making shell casings for ammunition. This information may even have been passed on to German Intelligence by the Nazi spy and propagandist William Joyce – better known as Lord Haw-Haw – who lived briefly in Tiger Bay during this period. Joyce was eventually caught, and became the only Englishman to be hanged for treason after the war.

The Basseys may well have been forced to leave the Bay because in Henry's absence Eliza Jane could simply no longer afford the rent on Bute Street, and from this point on the family received National Assistance. The Basseys were rehoused by Cardiff Council, who moved them a couple of miles inland, to the steel-working suburb of Splott. Here they lived at 132 Portmanmoor Road, close to the Dowlais steel mills. The entire street was demolished many years ago, and is now an industrial estate – but it's reasonable to assume the Basseys' house would have been like the majority of other dwellings in the area: two-up, two-down terraced houses that are not exactly small, but which would still have been extremely cramped for a family of their size. It's a fair bet that Shirley would have had little or no privacy until after she left home.

In Tiger Bay the Basseys had not been that unusual a family, but Splott was an all-white area, where they stood out from the crowd. For Shirley, her colour had never been an issue (and still isn't), as she once commented: 'My mother was white, so I never thought I was anything else.' In her first years in Splott, she was probably not conscious of any problems, but when she began attending the local Moorland Road Junior School at the age of five, Shirley personally encountered racism for the first time. There were several children at her school who called Shirley a 'nigger' or a 'darkie' to her face – but from all accounts, the ones who did so quickly received a real walloping from her, and thus learnt to leave her alone. As she later commented, describing her early years touring England as a singer, 'I'm a rat. You must never corner a rat because she will go for your throat. I would punch someone out if they had a go at me. I had a reputation in the nightclubs. People learnt not to cross me.' Perhaps because she took this stand early on, she's since claimed that she wasn't ever conscious of an atmosphere of racism in the area.

But if Shirley was able to defend herself in the playground, she and her sister Marina were vulnerable in the street during their 10-minute walk to school, and were often taunted by groups of local boys. Whenever Eliza Jane witnessed one of these incidents, she'd rush out of the house and give the youths a severe – and colourful – talking-to. Muriel Burgess quotes the Basseys' neighbour in Splott, Ifor Harry, as saying: 'I really admired Mrs Bassey, she was a remarkable lady. You see, it was an all-white school, and we know that children can be cruel. Mrs Bassey tried her best, but I think it was a nasty shock to the little girl.' Even 10 years later 'coloured' people were still a rarity in the area; a school photograph taken when Shirley was 14 shows her to be one of only two black girls in a sea of white faces.

To add to her social problems, Shirley was also visibly a lot poorer than most of her schoolmates, whose fathers mainly earned a decent living at the steel mill. Shirley, on the other hand, was still sleeping with her sisters three to a bed and wearing their hand-me-down clothing. The Basseys subsisted on National Assistance of £2 10/- per week – just under £300 in today's terms, but with seven children to feed it wouldn't have gone that far. The older girls, Gracie and Ella, were now both working in Cardiff, and thus able to contribute a little towards the household expenses, and the family income also rose somewhat when – despite their already cramped conditions – Eliza Jane took in another Nigerian sailor, Mr Mendi, as a lodger. Eventually he became far more than that to Eliza Jane, and her neighbours soon began referring to her as Mrs Mendi.

If Splott was a thriving area in the 1940s, it has evidently suffered a downturn of fortunes in recent decades, and local unemployment has taken a visible toll. Since both her childhood homes have been demolished, the one remaining landmark from Shirley's childhood still standing is Moorland Road School, which Shirley attended until she was 15. It's a slightly modernist – and quite large – structure dating from the 1920s or 1930s, and was probably very impressive when Shirley was a pupil there. Today, although still functioning as a school, it's in a somewhat dilapidated condition. The school is situated right next to the local library – an attractive Victorian building, which is sadly now completely derelict and boarded up.

At school, Shirley didn't really shine academically, but she was good at sports, especially Welsh baseball. Much later it was discovered that she'd suffered from childhood anaemia, possibly the result of receiving poor nutrition during the years of wartime and post-war food rationing. Even so, Shirley recalls that she was 'a happy kid, oh yes,' and despite the fact that it was wartime, 'my mother made sure we didn't go without anything. I had so much freedom.' Yet most of her siblings were much older than her, and she once commented: 'I was alone when I was a child. I never really had anything in common with my brother and sisters.'

Given that they didn't really fit in in Splott, it's unsurprising that the Bassey family continued to do much of their socializing in Tiger Bay, a short bus ride away, and Shirley spent much of her childhood leisure time there; from the age of seven onwards she would go to the Rainbow Club in Bute Street, where she took lessons in tap-dancing. Unfortunately, she was never able to display her tap-dancing skills in public, because the club's organizers discovered her talent for singing, and so 'every time there was a show, I had to sing. I was furious.' Describing her childhood in an interview in the *Telegraph* in 2003, she recalled: 'I was left to run wild. Terrible tom-boy. Always climbing trees. Maybe I didn't feel feminine enough to be with the girls. And then, in my late teens, I learnt to become more feminine as a way of controlling men. Girls can't help but flirt. When you wear your first bra you look down and say, "Oh, look at these." Actually, I wasn't very well-developed at first – slim little thing, no boobs . . . I was a loner. I didn't really need friends. I could be among people and still be alone in my own little world. I was a peculiar child. I am a peculiar grown-up.'

Clothes rationing was also still in place during Shirley's childhood. Tired of always having to wear cast-offs from her elder sisters, she dreamed of having her own new clothes, perhaps even of working in a gown shop when she grew up. But she had so many ambitions back then, as she told *Gay Times* journalist Vicky Powell: 'I wanted to be a nurse, but when I saw blood, that was the end of my nursing career. I wanted to be a stewardess, but I couldn't speak any languages. Then I wanted to be a model, but I wasn't tall enough.' On another occasion she recalled, 'I wanted to be so many things, almost anything but part of show business. It wasn't one of those things when you're seven and you're watching the film your mother has taken you to and you say that's it, I'm going to be an actress or I'm going to be a singer. It never entered my head. Honestly.'

This seems a little hard to believe, given the youthful age at which Shirley began performing: 'As a kid of eight I sang at the neighbours' weddings. They used to give me a slice of cake or a threepenny bit as a reward. But I was so shy, I would insist on singing from under the table where no one could see me.' It seems that music was always a key part of her world, as she recalled on another occasion: 'I would follow my sisters around. They would say, "Oh please, Mum, tell Shirley to get out of the way." I suppose singing was a way of getting noticed. No one else in my family sang. In the middle of the night, if I was unhappy, I wouldn't cry, I would sing, and my sisters would shout down to my mother, "Please make her stop." I was in my own world when I was singing. This skinny kid with the huge voice.' The sheer power of her voice was noticeable even then; in the school choir she began by singing in the front row, and was then moved backwards row by row, and then 'moved out of the room all together, because the voice was too powerful.'

The point at which Shirley became entranced by music (and probably began to daydream about it as a possible future career for herself) came when she was 13 or 14 years old, when she went on a school day trip to London, and saw her first live concert at the London Palladium. The star act was the American singer Jo Stafford, whom Shirley later recalled 'sang this incredible song out of tune. On purpose. I thought, gosh she must know music very well to do that.' Around the same time one of Shirley's sisters took her to see Billy Eckstine at Cardiff's New Theatre, and Shirley was hooked for life, although she later maintained that she 'had never been interested in show business until that point.'

Eckstine was also a favourite of Shirley's brother Henry, especially his duets with Sarah Vaughan. Shirley later stated that Henry was 'crazy about music', and it was through his record collection that she gained her first real education in the art of great singing. Although Shirley once said that no one else in her family sang, Henry seems to have enjoyed singing and the two of them would sing along with their idols: 'He used to do Billy Eckstine and I used to do Sarah Vaughan. I was only about 14 at the time, but my voice used to come out more Billy Eckstine than Sarah Vaughan. Sarah was another singer with a fantastic technique, but as a jazz singer, Ella Fitzgerald was the best for me.' Other favourites were Frankie Laine, Lena Horne and Johnny Mathis . . . although as far as male singers went, Shirley considered Frank Sinatra 'way out in front. Incredible. This man holds notes longer than anyone I know.' But if one had to point to one key record Shirley discovered in Henry's collection that cemented her love of music, it would have to be Judy Garland's 'Somewhere Over The Rainbow'; when she first heard it, Shirley would recall, 'Something went off in my head and my whole body. For me she is the greatest.' Little did she dream then that within a few years she would not only meet Judy in person, but that her heroine would end up giving her shrewd career advice (which basically amounted to: stick with your instincts, and don't be swayed by your advisers).

It was through listening to all these other singers and attempting to emulate them that Shirley first taught herself to sing properly; in the process she also developed her own breathing techniques, which later led many of her musical directors to believe that she'd been professionally trained, although she hadn't. In fact, Shirley couldn't have afforded singing lessons in those days even if she'd wanted them. In the event, she never took any formal singing lessons at all, and she didn't even practise any vocal exercises until the late 1980s. Consequently, and like many other singers, she encountered problems when she first began singing professionally, frequently losing her voice because she was unaccustomed to using it so much. Nor has she ever learnt to read music, but she's managed just fine throughout her career despite this.

When Shirley was still only 13 or 14, someone who'd heard her singing at a friend's party asked her to sing at a concert party he was throwing. Shirley told him that she couldn't possibly sing in public, but he eventually talked her into going through with it, and remembers that she sang 'Jezebel' there. Having overcome her reticence, almost immediately afterwards Shirley began singing in various dockland pubs as the vocalist with a trio of local boys (on piano, guitar and saxophone), despite being too young even to legally *be* in a pub. Her pub audiences were hard ones to please, as Shirley's schoolmate Margaret Baird later recalled: 'It could be tough. They threw things if they didn't like you and the applause was rare. And even if they did like you they didn't clap, they just didn't throw anything.' Through these performances Shirley was able to earn the occasional pound for herself – the equivalent of about £20 today – but the group constantly had to keep a lookout for approaching policemen, so that the underage Shirley could be hidden away in time. She was also still regularly attending the Rainbow Club, where she became part of a loosely organised group of local girls who'd taught themselves to sing in harmony as they danced, and who had named themselves the Bay Girls.

During the summer of 1951 Shirley and her classmates went to Porthcawl Camp for a week's school-trip holiday, and while there Shirley regularly sang to entertain her friends. Another schoolmate, Doreen Bentley, told Muriel Burgess: 'Years later I was at one of her concerts, one of those huge affairs with more than a thousand people, and I had exactly the same feeling all over again. The audience were showering Shirley with their love. And I thought that even then, when she was 14, Shirley must have felt our love. So this is how Shirley gets her fix, I thought. This is how she gets all the love she needs.'

Shirley Bassey left school at the end of the Christmas term 1951; since she turned 15 (then the official school-leaving age) at the beginning of January, she never went back again. Another schoolmate, Jeanette Cockley, recalled that on her last day of school Shirley 'went into every classroom and sang "This Is My Mother's Day".' Many of her schoolmates never saw her again after that day. Shirley was out in the world now.

t w o

THE BAY GIRL

At the beginning of 1952 Shirley went to work in the packing department of Currans, an enamelware factory located in a Tiger Bay back street where her sister Marina was already working. The premises were divided into two halves: a workshop where pots and pans were dipped in enamel, and the packing shed, where the enamelware was packed into boxes ready for dispatch to shops all over the country. Staff in the packing shed were all-female, with a male supervisor, and like factory staff everywhere in those days they listened to radio shows like *Music While You Work* and *Workers' Playtime* while they packed the pots and pans. Shirley was almost certainly not the only one who sang along with the hits of the day, but her powerful voice would probably have made her the most noticeable, and when the radio was switched off she was also known to sing requests for her fellow workers. '"Jezebel" was their favourite,' she later recalled, 'although the supervisor was always telling me to stop.' To supplement her Currans wages of £3 per week (nearly £180 in today's terms), Shirley also sometimes sang in the local working men's clubs, but this was confined strictly to weekends only, 'when the women were invited.' She could now afford to buy her own clothes, and still vividly remembers the first dress she bought: 'It was tartan, with a big skirt that rustled. I wore it to the factory dance, and was in heaven.'

By now Shirley already knew that she didn't want to be packing pots for the rest of her life, and she had no doubts at all about what she should be doing instead. 'I knew I had talent. I was given it – we're all given something and you should use it, so I used it,' she later explained. She took part in every song contest she could, in any town within easy reach of Cardiff, but her first 'professional' solo appearance took place virtually on her own doorstep, at the Splott Social and Athletic Club in Portmanmoor Road. Ever since it had played host to some radical left-wing speakers, legend has it that the club had become much better known locally as 'The Bomb & Dagger', named for the traditional equipment of the anarchist (and probably inspired by the way they were depicted in newspaper cartoons).

The Currans girls encouraged Shirley to audition for a singing spot on the BBC Wales radio show *Welsh Rarebit*, which showcased local talent. Shirley contacted the show, and was granted an appointment; when the day came, she duly turned up at the BBC's studio in Cardiff, and performed Harold Arlen's song 'Stormy Weather' accompanied by the show's in-house pianist. The song dated back to Harlem's famous Cotton Club in the 1930s and had since been mainly associated with Billie Holiday and Lena Horne (who had sung it in the 1943 film of the same name). It was a bold choice for an inexperienced young singer to pick, since both Holiday and Horne are pretty hard acts to follow. But according to Muriel Burgess, the song may have been a bad choice, simply because the show's female producer Mai Jones didn't care for it at all – and Jones apparently also wasn't impressed by the fact that Shirley couldn't read music. The show's link man Wyn Calvin tried to cushion the blow of rejection by telling Shirley that her youth was against her, and that she would almost certainly be turned down because of it – but also that she should try again in a few months, after she'd gained some more experience. Nevertheless, the fact remained, and it must have hurt: Shirley had failed the audition.

As so often happens, Shirley's first big professional break came about almost by chance. After she'd performed one Saturday night at a working men's club in Cardiff's Paradise Place she met the local booking agent Georgie Wood. Wood had liked Shirley's voice, and asked her to audition for a touring theatrical revue show that he was helping to cast, called *Memories of Jolson*, which was based on the life of the 1930s 'jazz singer' Al Jolson. In this, Wood was acting on behalf of the London-based theatrical agent Sidney Burns, who had recently discovered that 'coloured' variety shows were proving extremely popular with theatregoers, and consequently wanted to mount one of his own. Since there simply weren't that many black entertainers at all in Britain in those days, the clubs of Tiger Bay were an obvious place for Burns to begin recruiting.

Wood also told Shirley at their first meeting that he was also planning to audition all the other Bay Girls, but Shirley was the only one he personally invited (the others simply turned up at the audition, having heard about it through the grapevine). Apart from Shirley, the chorus line of Bay Girls that were eventually chosen for the show comprised Iris Freeman, Mahalia Davies, Robina Ali, Maureen Jommet and Margaret and Daphne Freeman.

The auditions took place a few days later at Frenchie's Annexe Studio in Bute Street. Walter French was a local entrepreneur, a West African, whose nightclub Frenchie's was very popular with American GIs during the Second World War; his other Tiger Bay venue the Annexe was where Saturday-night dances were held, and where Shirley had also taken some tap-dancing lessons as a child. After he'd seen them all perform, Georgie Wood told the Bay Girls that he was sending them to London for a final audition with the show's star – who was also the only white person in the cast – a British singer with the memorable name of Eddie Reindeer.

With this audition on the horizon, Shirley decided it would be sensible to give in her notice at Currans, since she might have to leave for London at a moment's notice. Currans' personnel officer Stephen Shepherd had always encouraged Shirley to pursue her musical ambitions, and she retained fond memories of the firm, as she recalled in recent years: 'I was happy there. I had a great time. Every Thursday there was the factory club: archery, darts, dancing. I was happy until success entered my life, then it was downhill. Success spoilt me. It took away my happiness. There were so many demands put upon me. I will be happy again when I retire.'

But after she left Currans, weeks went past with no word from London, and then the weeks turned into months, and the call to audition still hadn't arrived. Shirley must have been extremely nervous about her financial position, as well as feeling slightly foolish in case this opportunity had simply fallen through. But this kind of delay was nothing unusual in the theatrical world, and the audition call did eventually arrive. So the Bay Girls all travelled to London, and met with Reindeer in some rehearsal rooms opposite

Soho's famous Windmill Theatre. They performed 'Walking My Baby Back Home' in a fairly ragged manner, but Reindeer seemed content enough. He also asked to hear Shirley singing on her own, and was impressed enough with her performance to promise her a solo spot in the show. The girls all then returned to Cardiff for a week – much of which was taken up with celebratory parties – before coming back to London to begin rehearsing in earnest.

In June 1953 *Memories Of Jolson* finally opened at the Grand Theatre in Luton, with shows taking place twice nightly (for which Shirley earned a salary of £10 per week, which amounts to roughly £550 in today's terms). Also taking part in the show were the Ben Johnson Ballet, a coloured dance troupe. The West Indian Johnson had founded his dance company in 1951; it consisted of five dancers, including Johnson and his wife Pamela Winter, who unofficially acted as 'mother' to the troupe of inexperienced Bay girls.

The opening night must have seemed somewhat less than magical to Shirley and the other girls. The scenery was old and tattered, and the trunk of stage costumes hadn't arrived in time for the first night's performance, so the cast had to go on stage wearing their own clothes. When the costumes finally arrived the next day, they were as old and tatty as the scenery, and had to be held together with safety pins. According to Muriel Burgess, Shirley's pinned-up gown started to come apart on stage – though according to Shirley herself this incident may have happened much earlier on, at one of her first bookings 'at a club near my home'. At this point Shirley 'didn't have any glamorous clothes, but I did manage to get my hands on a bustier, which was black, strapless, lacy and it was lovely. It was meant to be worn underneath, but I didn't care.' One of the girls loaned her a lavender net long skirt; and from another girl she got an elastic belt with a big buckle to complete her costume. 'And that's how I went on stage . . . that was my first Bassey dress. That was my only outfit. And eventually the belt was giving . . . I was doing "Stormy Weather" and put up my arms to do a big note and the belt pinged off and the skirt fell down!' Grabbing her skirt, Shirley ran off stage, and was later berated by the stage manager, who insisted that if she'd been a real professional she would have stayed on stage no matter what happened. Recounting this incident on Graham Norton's TV show, Shirley elaborated, insisting that her response to the stage manager had been: 'But I had no knickers on!' The same manager had apparently also suggested that she should change her name, but she had refused to even entertain the idea: 'There was no way I was going to do that. If I became famous, I wanted all my school mates to know it was me.'

Asked in 2003 what the 16-year-old Shirley Bassey was actually like, Dame Shirley replied: 'She was very stubborn. She wouldn't listen to reason. And she was very shy. Still is, in a way. I do a lot of things to cover up shyness. I talk loudly.'

After its run in Luton, *Memories of Jolson* went on tour, to Coventry and Salford and further afield, and quickly settled into a routine. The company played two shows each day from Monday to Saturday; Sundays were spent travelling to the next town on the itinerary. Everywhere the girls went they stayed in theatrical boarding houses, where Shirley usually shared a room with Iris Freeman. Rather than eat the landladies' exorbitantly priced dinners, the girls usually had a whip-round and cooked a communal meal on Pam

Winter's primus stove. Understandably, Shirley would go out to dinner as often as nice young men asked her to, which was often.

Although *Memories of Jolson* undoubtedly opened doors for Shirley, it wasn't an experience that she particularly enjoyed, as she recalled decades later: 'I was the little soubrette and left after two months. I was the youngest in the show and there was a lot of bitchiness from the other girls. I didn't like that. There was only one white man in the show and I had to sing a duet with him. It was a Jolson number; 'By the Light of the Silvery Moon', I think. All the black people were supposed to be cotton pickers. Can you imagine? The English, what do we know about slavery? Although they do say the English started it.'

The show finally closed in November, but instead of returning home straight away, Shirley managed to get bookings for several solo shows, including two concerts at the NCO Club in Burtonwood in late December, for which she was paid £10.

Immediately afterwards she travelled back to Splott, laden with presents, to celebrate Christmas with her family. In January she turned 17.

*

Another London-based promoter who had noticed the popularity of 'coloured' shows was the agent Joe Collins (the father of actress Joan and novelist Jackie), who was about to launch his own touring revue, *Hot From Harlem*. The music for this show was to be American swing from the Cotton Club era, and it was intended to feature an all-black cast of British performers. Collins was having great difficulty in casting the soubrette for the show, until the

Jolson promoter Sidney Burns recommended that he should get in touch with Shirley. After a brief interview at Collins's office in London, Shirley was given the part without her even having to sing a note, as Collins recounted in his autobiography: 'She was just a skinny little thing in her mid-teens, yet I sensed she had stage presence and could be made to look stylish. I did not bother to hear her sing. I reckoned that even if she wasn't much as a vocalist, she would fit my show if she were dressed the way I had in mind.'

To make sure that Shirley looked the part, Collins hired the fashion designer Douglas Darnell to design her gowns and make sure that she looked 'feline and seductive.' Darnell had already designed dresses for both Joan Collins and Diana Dors – the two biggest British sex symbols of the era. Shirley later described the first gown Darnell designed for her as being 'sexy, and it was heavy because it was all diamanté.' Though neither of them could have guessed it at the time, this was to be the start of a long and extremely fruitful relationship, as Darnell became Shirley's principal costume designer, usually producing several gowns a year for her over the next 50 years. As time went on, Shirley grew more confident in telling Darnell what she wanted, as he recalled in 2003: 'She tells me what she was thinking. I sketch it. She says, "I don't like that." And then we have a row.' In the same interview Shirley then countered, 'We take one thing from one sketch and put it on another. Between us we get the look.' In fact, many of the gowns Darnell designed went through several stages of evolution, as simple dresses acquired elaborate additions and extensions, so that their later incarnations were often almost unrecognizable from their simpler beginnings.

But as a teenager Shirley was still unsure about her ability to project glamour, though she had always known that this was an ability possessed by her sister Grace: 'She was my favourite sister, and she was so glamorous. She used to wear cami-knickers with a little camisole top and a suspender belt and she was ever so careful with her stockings – she'd put them on with gloves. To watch her getting dressed was a delight.'

As her confidence grew, Shirley's stage costumes became more and more dramatic, a deliberate choice, as she later explained: 'Of course, the whole stage thing is showing off. The fact that I walk on in front of thousands of people and sing, that's showing off to begin with, so why not do it in a spectacular gown?' Over the first few years of her stage career Shirley also gradually refined her stage make-up, partly through trial-and-error experimentation and partly through advice from others, until she was finally happy with it. In her youth Shirley suffered from bad skin and acne, which she'd cover up with beauty spots before going on stage. She's claimed that her skin was so bad that she once went on stage wearing no less than six beauty spots.

Several other Bay Girls appeared in *Hot From Harlem*, but Shirley was the only one who sang three solo songs, including 'Ebb Tide'. In the five months she spent working on *Hot From Harlem* Shirley toured most of England and Wales, and was paid £18 a week, or roughly £940 in present day terms. If that seems well-paid, bear in mind that it works out to only £1 10/- (£78) per show. 'You might say I got a bargain,' Joe Collins concluded, adding that, 'Shirley Bassey put the heat into *Hot From Harlem* . . . fingers snapping, hips working overtime, she was a right little tease, with a seductive, growling voice. Sometimes the wolf-whistles from the audience drowned her singing. Both the audience <u>and</u> the cast went wild over her.' In local reviews Shirley was already being described as 'England's answer to Lena Horne'; when the show played at Cardiff's New Theatre, the audience included a large contingent from her family, friends and neighbours. She had come home in triumph.

But in April 1954 Shirley left the tour early, several months before its run was due to end. The reason was that she was five months' pregnant, and it was becoming impossible to hide it any longer. So she went home to Cardiff. 'Eliza Jane wasn't best pleased, but what could she do?' Shirley later recalled. Once back home Shirley attempted to audition once again for BBC Wales, but the fact that she was visibly pregnant – and worse, unmarried as well – ruled out any chance of her wish being granted. Instead, she happened to see a sign saying 'waitress wanted' in the window of a Greek restaurant in Cardiff's Frederick Street, applied for the job and got it. She'd later refer to her work there by the American slang term 'slinging hash' – but she also enjoyed it, and remained working at the restaurant until just before the birth of her daughter that September.

Shirley named the girl Sharon, and insisted on keeping her. It's hard to convey now just how scandalous this was at the time. Single mothers were then almost completely ostracized socially; they were regarded as 'fallen women', and usually forced to give up their children for adoption – but even if this course were taken, a girl's 'reputation' could still be ruined, and she was often forced to move away and begin a new life elsewhere, where her guilty secret was not known. Shirley, however, dealt with the issue head on, although she attempted to keep her baby's existence a secret from most of her professional contacts. 'The baby was a secret,' she later admitted. 'Not many people knew about it because I can be very private, just as I can be very public. But I could look after myself.'

Not only was Shirley not married to her baby's father, but she has always resolutely refused to name him, a position she maintains to this day: 'I don't talk about it for this reason: Sharon gets touchy if I mention it and I understand that.' It wasn't until 1998 – after a court case in which she had denied charges that she was anti-Semitic – that Shirley revealed that Sharon's father was Jewish, that he had been married with two children at the time of their affair, and that she had never told him of Sharon's existence: 'It would hurt too many people.'

After Sharon was born, Shirley returned to her waitressing job, and remained there throughout the winter of 1954/55, while Eliza looked after Sharon at home. Although her pregnancy had been the reason why Shirley had quit show business, she was also disillusioned with it. She'd found touring around Britain to be a miserable business – she had hated the travelling, the shabby digs she'd been forced to stay in and half the people she toured with, and she'd often been prone to severe homesickness. As she later put it, until leaving home she'd 'led a fairly sheltered life, and it was scary to be out in the world.' Now she was back at home with her family, and she saw no reason to ever leave again – but although she didn't know it, her waitressing days would soon be coming to an end.

three

THE MANAGER

Michael Sullivan had show business in his blood, almost literally; both his mother and grandmother had been professional actresses, and his great-great-uncle was Sir Arthur Sullivan, the musical half of the Gilbert & Sullivan partnership. Michael's career began at the age of 14, when he took a job as an office boy with a theatrical agency; within three years he had become 'the youngest theatrical agent in London.' In 1955, the year he met Shirley Bassey, he was 33 years old and had an agency of his own which had 72 acts on its books and controlled the bookings for 23 variety theatres. In addition to this, Sullivan was also producing his own touring shows, revues, pantomimes and ice spectaculars. Unfortunately, by this point television ownership was starting to become widespread in Britain, and as a result many theatres were suffering a serious decline in attendance. One theatre chain had gone bankrupt owing Sullivan £2,000 (an absolute fortune in those days, equivalent to around £100,000 today), and he was deeply in debt himself – but he was still in business, and determined to overcome these obstacles.

At the beginning of 1955, Sullivan was approached by the Little

Theatre in Jersey to find them a small dance company for a two-week booking in March. Sullivan suggested the Ben Johnson Ballet, and the theatre agreed. But since the dancers couldn't stay on stage for an entire show, Sullivan suggested that they find a singer to perform in front of the curtains while they changed sets and costumes backstage. He had no one specific in mind, however, and one of Johnson's dancers suggested that he should approach a singer they'd worked with in the *Memories of Jolson* show – Shirley Bassey. After they'd told Sullivan a bit about her, he agreed to give Shirley an audition and to pay her train fare to London.

Shortly afterwards Shirley received a telegram from Ben Johnson, offering her the Jersey booking, subject to audition. Her immediate reaction was to say no, but her mother – who had always encouraged Shirley in her musical career – eventually persuaded her that this was too good an opportunity to let slip by her, and that at the very least she should go to London for the audition and see how things developed from there. The Bassey family agreed between them that Shirley's sister Iris and her husband Bill should look after baby Sharon while Shirley was in London, and that they should continue to do so if Shirley ended up going to Jersey. Although she agreed to this, Shirley found the idea of leaving Sharon the hardest aspect of all this to deal with, as she later recalled: 'I wasn't sorry when I had to leave *Hot From Harlem*, and I wasn't sorry when I went to work in the Greek restaurant, but I was very sorry when I had to leave little Sharon and go to London for that audition. She was only six months old. I *hated* leaving her. When I got to London I spent all my money on phone calls to my sister to see if the baby was all right.'

But go to London she did, and on the evening of 14 February 1955 Shirley met Michael Sullivan for the first time. When he arrived at the Max Rivers rehearsal rooms in Great Newport Street, Shirley was sitting on the floor, wearing a yellow sweater and old blue jeans, and Sullivan wasn't particularly impressed by the way she looked. Then Ben Johnson – who was rehearsing there with his wife and Louise Benjamin – introduced Shirley to Sullivan, who asked her what she was planning to sing. Shirley was obviously nervous, and practically hid behind the piano for the whole of her performance – but when she launched into 'Stormy Weather', accompanied by pianist Stanley Myers, Sullivan experienced 'an uncanny spine-tingling sensation.' He'd seen thousands of singers audition in his time, but none that had ever affected him in this way, and he couldn't explain it. Afterwards, the dancers, Sullivan and Shirley all adjourned to a nearby pub, where Sullivan offered Shirley the Jersey booking and she accepted – although she was still nervous and her confidence seemed low. To boost her self-esteem, Sullivan promised Shirley that he would fly out to Jersey at some point to see her perform.

It was a promise that he hadn't really intended to keep, but over the next few weeks Sullivan found that he was unable to get this girl singer out of his head. He flew to Jersey to see the show's opening night. In the interludes between dance numbers Shirley came on stage to sing 'Stormy Weather', 'Ebb Tide', 'Smile' and 'Sunny Side of the Street' (according to Muriel Burgess, she also sang 'By the Light of the Silvery Moon' while dancing with Ben Johnson).

Sullivan wasn't at all impressed by Shirley's appearance, since at this point she possessed 'no sense of make-up' and was wearing a hideous green dress that she'd apparently bought for her sister's wedding. Her stagecraft was also pretty much non-existent – she was stiff and awkward, and didn't even smile at the audience once. Even so, Sullivan discovered that Shirley still sent shivers down his spine every time she sang. He was fast becoming convinced that there was something special about this girl, a raw talent that might pay off in a big way, if it could only be polished. Even in those racially insensitive days he felt that Shirley's colour shouldn't be a problem, since the mainstream public had long since accepted the likes of Lena Horne and Eartha Kitt. Sullivan began to think seriously about the possibilities of managing Shirley, of teaching her everything he'd learned about the stage, of moulding this scrawny girl into a real star. He knew it would require vast amounts of work on his part, but he felt that it might just be worth it in the long term. Thinking he might be deluding himself about Shirley's talent, however, Sullivan sought a second opinion from the Jersey booker Sydney James, who was also in the audience. Nevertheless, when the distinctly unenthusiastic James revealed that he was unimpressed with Shirley, Sullivan decided to ignore James's opinion and go with his first instincts.

After the show, in the bar of the hotel in St Helier where he, Shirley and the dancers were all staying, Sullivan told Shirley that he wanted to become her manager, and that he thought he could make her into a star. Shirley immediately began to cry. Even at this early stage in her career she had already been told too many lies by would-be managers, promoters and agents, had been made too many promises that had led absolutely nowhere, and she was deeply disillusioned about the glamour of show business. Moved by her tears, Sullivan took Shirley by the hand and led her upstairs to his hotel room.

Sullivan was a self-confessed womanizer, and even though he was at this point on his third marriage (he would eventually marry five times), he had never been really capable of fidelity, nor did it matter to him. In his autobiography, Sullivan claims that on that night in Jersey he and Shirley slept together, for the first and only time, and that the 'doubting, insecure girl from Tiger Bay was a tigress in her own right'; he also claims that she scratched his back so badly during their lovemaking that he had to stay away from home for an extra five days afterwards, until the scratches had healed, to prevent his wife Juhni from finding out about this affair. Sullivan may have flown to nearby Guernsey, where Leonard 'Berry' Beresford Cooke, one of his main financiers, lived. If he was going to manage this girl, he would need some capital to invest in her training. Sullivan also speculated in his book that if the sexual side of his relationship with Shirley had continued, he might have remained her manager for decades. There's no reason to believe this view is correct – perhaps we should rather put it down to simple vanity: he was, after all, nearly twice Shirley's age at this point.

After the Jersey show had finished its run and Shirley had returned to the mainland, Sullivan was surprised when the days and weeks went past with no phone call from Shirley. He asked Ben Johnson to contact her, and a meeting was set up – but because of crossed wires, both sides failed to show up. After much confusion, Shirley finally met with Sullivan in his apartment at London's Mapleton Hotel, where he was lying in bed with a bad case of flu.

Sullivan's wife Juhni wasn't at all impressed with her husband's new 'star' discovery, especially since Shirley had shown up wearing 'a transparent raincoat over a salmon-pink dress.' ('Wait until you hear her sing,' Sullivan told Juhni after Shirley had gone).

Sullivan offered to put Shirley under a management contract and to pay her a weekly wage, whether she performed in public or not – but in order to earn that she would have to rehearse for four hours a day until he decided that she was ready to appear on stage in public again. In addition, Sullivan said that he'd pay for all Shirley's stage costumes, a pianist and rehearsal rooms, her music, her publicity and all her travelling expenses. He would also arrange her accommodation in London, above Olivelli's in Store Street, just off Tottenham Court Road. Olivelli's was an Italian restaurant which rented the rooms above it exclusively to theatrical people, so Shirley would have at least some contact with kindred spirits, and not feel completely isolated in the big city. Shirley, however, expressed some doubts about continuing in show business at all, and in particular told Sullivan that the experience of touring had made her absolutely miserable. This time would be different, Sullivan assured her. When she was finally ready to tour again, it would only be himself and a pianist that would travel with her, and they would always stay in decent hotels. On those terms, Shirley agreed to Sullivan becoming her manager, and he told her he would have a contract drawn up and ready for her to sign within a week.

After Shirley had left, Juhni still thought that her husband might be making a hideous mistake by taking this girl on as a protégée, so Sullivan promised her that he would seek out a few other opinions about Shirley from those who had already worked with her. Which he did, only to learn that promoter Sidney Burns was fairly scathing about Shirley's lack of experience, while Joe Collins was still angry that Shirley had walked out on *Hot From Harlem* before the end of the show's run, which he thought highly unprofessional of her. Sullivan never passed these negative opinions of Shirley on to Juhni, but instead told her that both men had praised the singer highly.

A few days later Sullivan summoned Shirley to his office, where he gave her a copy of the draft contract which he'd prepared; it ran for six months' duration, with renewal options that could extend it for a further five years. Sullivan told her to take the contract away and discuss it with her mother; since the age of majority was 21 in those days, Shirley was still a minor at this point, and Eliza's approval of the deal was legally required.

When Shirley returned to London a week later with her mother's blessing, she was ready to sign Sullivan's contract – but first the agent tackled her on a couple of points that concerned him. He asked her whether she had signed any previous contracts with anyone else, and she admitted that she did have a prior arrangement with a booking agency, which had been signed by her mother – but since that agency had not found Shirley any work for a long time, she considered their relationship to be at an end. Sullivan then revealed that Joe Collins had told him all about her leaving the run of *Hot From Harlem* prematurely; he wanted to know the reason why, and also why she hadn't told him about all this before now. At this point Shirley broke down, and told Sullivan all about leaving the tour because of her pregnancy. After she'd given birth to Sharon, she'd tried to get more singing work through her agency, but they'd offered her nothing. Sullivan asked her about the child's father, but Shirley refused to divulge his name, and said that she hadn't seen him since before the baby was born. Knowing how highly scandalous illegitimacy was considered in those days, Sullivan was well aware that this news could end Shirley's career before it had even begun. He agreed to help her keep the baby's existence a secret – but he also warned her that if she ever did become famous, the newspapers would start digging for dirt. If they did, they would be sure to find out about the baby very quickly, and they'd make a very public meal of her hidden secret.

Shirley and Sullivan both signed the contract, and she spent the next three months in constant rehearsals with pianist Bob Wardlaw. Additionally, Sullivan gave her extra coaching in how to phrase a lyric, and in all the tricks he had learned about stagecraft over the years: how to make an entrance and an exit, how to project the voice and how to make eye contact with the audience and hold their attention. 'After the first 16 bars of a song their attention begins to wander,' he told her. 'Until then they are busy taking you in. That's when you have to get them and hold them. Take them one side at a time and let your eyes go from the front to the middle to the back. You don't have to move much and when you get a high note, throw your head back and give it to the people upstairs. That way you get all of them and keep them.' Shirley subsequently incorporated all Sullivan's advice into her live performance, where it's still evident to this day. He also encouraged her to develop her own vocal style, rather than rely on emulating her musical heroes.

Meanwhile, Shirley was costing Sullivan a lot of money. He was paying her a wage of £10 a week (about £480 today), plus the occasional £1 bonus so she could enjoy a night out. In addition, the rehearsal studio cost £1 per day to rent, and Bob Wardlaw was also being paid £12 per week. It was a hefty investment, and thus quite a gamble by the already financially stretched Sullivan.

For the visual side of the act, Sullivan had decided that Shirley's new stage outfit (which was overseen by Juhni) should be a black velvet gown with elbow-length gloves. Shirley hated it, and refused point blank to wear it ('As soon as I put it on, I burst into tears. I was too young to wear black.'). She had wanted to wear much brighter colours, but in the end Sullivan got his way. He also made her wear a built-up hairpiece on stage, to increase her height.

For the debut appearance of the 'new' Shirley Bassey, Sullivan decided to go in at as high-profile a level as he could manage, booking her into the Hippodrome Theatre in Keighley, Yorkshire – where she would appear second on the bill. She was extremely nervous about this spotlight falling upon her, and although she got through the rehearsals in one piece, when it came to the actual performance she was 'near to panic', according to Sullivan. Standing in the wings, Sullivan pushed Shirley gently in the back and on to the stage as the house band struck up 'I Can't Give You Anything But Love', and she took the song – and the rest of her performance – in her stride, as if this were the thing that she was born to do. As she sang, Sullivan wandered slowly around the theatre, observing the audience reaction – and was immediately struck by the fact that all the old people there were applauding just as loudly as the young men. This fact convinced Sullivan that he had indeed backed the right horse: 'That was all the confirmation I needed of my faith in Shirley Bassey.'

After Keighley, Sullivan and Shirley took a two-week breather before her next stage appearance, in order for Sullivan to polish her act further and perfect her stage lighting. Shirley then undertook an 11-week tour of provincial theatres, and although she went down well in some towns, in Northampton and Guernsey she completely bombed, and Sullivan began to wonder if he hadn't made a ghastly mistake after all. It wasn't as if Shirley was earning much, either. Sullivan was being paid £35 per week for her appearances (approximately £1,700 today), out of which £18 went to Shirley, £12 went to the pianist and £3 10/- went in agent's commission. In addition to this, Sullivan had to pay their travelling expenses, as well as the costs of the music and Shirley's publicity photos. In short, the whole enterprise was operating at a loss.

Shirley, however, had become suspicious that Sullivan was exploiting her financially. To placate her fears, Sullivan allowed Shirley to collect her own cheque from the theatre, from which she was to deduct her own salary and then forward the balance on to him. This arrangement worked for a little while, but it wasn't too long before the cheques from Shirley stopped coming. After nothing had arrived for a month, Sullivan summoned Shirley to his office in London for a serious talking-to. When she arrived, Sullivan was both surprised and appalled to discover that a taste of applause had obviously turned his discovery's head, and her old lack of confidence had now been replaced by a bad case of youthful arrogance. Shirley began the meeting by acting in a high-handed manner, telling Sullivan, 'This is my money. I pay you.' Sullivan then patiently explained to her that this was not so; it was actually the complete opposite of the truth: he paid her, because he was promoting her. Frustrated and maddened by Shirley's attitude, Sullivan threatened to tear up their contract. She was just too much trouble, and not worth all the hard work he'd put in on her behalf. Faced with this possibility, Shirley promptly burst into tears, and Sullivan told her to come back and see him the next day. She should sleep on all that they'd discussed, and decide whether she wanted to continue their relationship on his terms, or not at all.

The following afternoon a very meek Shirley met with Sullivan again, and told him that she wanted to 'straighten things out.' She even called him 'Mr Sullivan.' She explained that she'd used all the missing money to pay off her previous agents, who had sued her for non-payment of back commission. Sullivan agreed to clear this debt for her, and to then deduct it in instalments from her wages. Their partnership had survived its first test, and they were back in business.

*

Either on her first national tour or shortly afterwards, Shirley was told by a promoter that he'd like to see whether she could handle playing at the Glasgow Empire. The theatre was notorious as one of the toughest places in the country for any entertainer to play, and its heckling audiences were legendary. 'I asked him why I had to go all the way to Glasgow to prove myself,' Shirley recalled decades later. 'He explained that, if I could win over that audience, he'd get me a contract to appear in all the Moss Empires around the UK.'

So Shirley agreed, and headed north to Glasgow. Her impressions of the merciless Empire audience were ones she would never forget: 'It was like a bear pit. I stood in the wings and heard them boo the acrobats when they nearly lost their balance, and boo the comedians when their jokes weren't funny enough. Oh, they were dreadful. I was petrified. But I told myself that that wasn't going to happen to me.' When Shirley's turn came to go on stage she was understandably nervous, but got through her first song without any incidents. The trouble started as she began singing her second number, a slow and sexy rendition of Cole Porter's 'I've Got You Under My Skin': 'The audience began hooting and hollering, and telling me to get my clothes off.' Instead of attempting to battle on regardless and ignore this onslaught, Shirley simply stopped singing; half a bar later, the theatre's orchestra also raggedly ground to a halt. The heckling slowly subsided, and the whole theatre was plunged into a nervous silence. 'At first I just stared at the audience,' Shirley recalled. 'Then I spoke into the microphone. "Now look here," I said, in a broad Welsh accent. "I've come here tonight to entertain you lot, and if you don't want to listen then I'll bloody well go home. But you can at least give me a chance".' The silence continued. 'Then I looked at the musical director, started tapping my foot and said, "Now!" Well, by the time I finished my final number, the applause was deafening.' News of the way that Shirley had handled the Glaswegian audience filtered back to Moss Empires, who kept their word and gave her a contract. 'I was a heroine,' she later said of the event. 'It was a career milestone.'

Of course, most performances didn't contain that much drama, and despite Sullivan's assurances Shirley still found touring a deeply draining experience. In his autobiography, Max Bygraves recalled an evening when – decades later – Shirley told him about her life on the road during the early days of her career:

> The drives up and down the A6 to one-night stands 'up North'. Hurrying to arrive in time to get the electric iron plugged in so she could press her crumpled dress. Then to rehearse with a band that, more often than not, 'couldn't tell A flat from a bull's foot'! And to win over tough audiences when she was still a teenager. This went on for dozens of nights, week in and week out. If she wanted to pay the rent and become known, there was no alternative.

Shirley always travelled with a portable record player and a pile of her favourite records, partly for her own entertainment, but also partly to demonstrate her musical wishes to orchestra leaders who would otherwise not have understood what she required. It was not an easy existence, as Shirley reminisced in 1998: 'I didn't go through my teenage years like any other teenager, with lots of boys coming round to pick you up and take you to the local dance. I missed all that.' She added wistfully that she still 'sort of dreams about that, I suppose.'

Muriel Burgess claims that during this period Shirley had an eight-month-long affair with the TV producer and film director Robert Hartford-Davis, and was deeply upset when he left the country and their relationship ended. Whether this is true or not, Shirley was certainly under a high degree of emotional stress. She worried constantly that Sharon would forget her, and that Iris would inevitably come to replace her in her daughter's affections – but there was nothing she could do about the situation. If she

wanted to carry on working, and she did – at least most of the time
– there was no other way things could be arranged.

Meanwhile, Sullivan knew that the theatre tours had taken
Shirley about as far as they possibly could; to reach any higher,
Sullivan was convinced, the key to Shirley's future lay in cabaret
performance. He duly made an appointment to meet with Bertie
Green, to try and get Shirley a booking in Green's famous night-
club, the Astor.

f o u r

THE RISING STAR

The Astor Club was a lavish nightclub designed for the sophisticated set, and was located at the southern end of Berkeley Square in London's Mayfair; Michael Sullivan would later describe its interior as a 'gilded cavern.' Since he feared that his reputation as an agent might suffer if he kept pushing this unknown singer he was managing (and he would need to remain in business as an agent if Shirley's career failed to take off), Sullivan recruited agent Sonny Zahl to actually strike the deal with Bertie Green for Shirley's Astor booking; after Zahl's negotiations, it was agreed that Shirley would be paid £65 per week for a two-week engagement at the club (just over £3,000 a week in today's money).

But once again, Sullivan would have many expenses to be taken into account. Convinced that Shirley needed at least some original material to perform before the Astor audience, Sullivan approached songwriter Ross Parker, who had written 'The Girl In The Alice Blue Gown' and 'There'll Always Be An England' (although for some reason Sullivan refers to Parker as 'Ross Taylor' in his autobiography). Sullivan took Parker to see Shirley singing live at a show in Chatham, after which Parker said that he would be happy to write some new songs for Shirley to sing, at his standard fee of two hundred guineas apiece (which is nearly £10,000 in modern terms). Despite being almost completely broke, Sullivan agreed.

The two men next went to the house of Sullivan's mother-in-law, because there was a piano there. Over the course of the next four hours, Parker played Sullivan all of his own songs, and the latter 'was so impressed that I wanted to manage him as a singer, but none of the songs he had sung seemed right for Shirley.' Sullivan told Parker that what he was looking for was, 'some bite in the lines, something saucy. I want her to sell sex.' Parker and he then discussed the nature of the Astor's regular clientele, and what subject matter they might relate to; they were rich socialites, the kind of people who would soon be called the 'jet-set.' They were the kind of people 'who burned the candle at both ends.'

With that idea as a springboard, Parker went off and wrote a song titled 'Burn My Candle'. The song would end up becoming Shirley's first single the following year, although its 'suggestive' lyrics ('Who's got a match worth striking ?') would promptly get it banned by the BBC. Sullivan candidly admitted to Parker that although he loved the song, he simply couldn't afford the 200 guinea asking price. Perhaps amused by Sullivan's sheer nerve in commisioning him, Parker agreed to negotiate a deal; they settled on a fee of £150 (the equivalent of just over £7,000 today), payable in ten instalments of £15. Having confided just how broke he was, Sullivan demonstrated that he truly possessed a silver tongue by somehow talking Parker into also acting as Shirley's accompanist during her engagement at the Tivoli Theatre in Hull, for a knock-down price of £25 per week (just over £1,000 in present-day terms). During the Hull run Parker also rehearsed Shirley in the new song each morning, and then even agreed to act as her accompanist for the Astor engagement as well (and for the same weekly fee), rather than trust in the club's house band to get his arrangements right.

For her Astor costume, Sullivan had Shirley fitted in a white gown that was figure-hugging down to the knee, then flared in folds down to the floor. On her first night at the club Shirley went on stage at one in the morning, and was a sensation from the start, with 'Burn My Candle' more than proving its worth as an audience-pleasing finale. The rest of Shirley's stint at the club went equally well.

One evening in the middle of the second week of her run Ross Parker called Sullivan to tell him that he'd heard a rumour that Jack Hylton would be visiting the Astor that night. Parker advised Sullivan to make sure that he was also present.

*

During the Big Band era of the 1930s and 1940s, Jack Hylton had been a well-known and successful musician, fronting his own orchestra. After the war he became a hugely successful impresario, owning several West End theatres as well as his own nightclub, the Albany, from where late-night music shows were now being broadcast on television. Hylton wanted to become more involved with this new medium, and when they met at the Astor that night Sullivan impressed him as someone who might be a useful assistant and ally. He was also impressed with Shirley as a singer – and as it happened, he desperately needed to find a decent singer in a hurry. Maria Pavlou, a Greek singer who was appearing in a show of his at the Adelphi Theatre, had suddenly been rushed to hospital with peritonitis; as a result, Hylton's show was now a performer short. Could Shirley possibly fill the gap, starting immediately? Sullivan agreed on the spot, and he and Hylton arranged to meet again in the morning to discuss the details, and other matters as well.

For it wasn't only Shirley Bassey that Hylton was interested in. By the end of their business meeting that morning, Sullivan had agreed to work for Jack Hylton as an agent, in the process merging his own agency with Hylton's. It seemed as if Sullivan's financial problems might finally be coming to an end, and he had found another important London showcase for Shirley's talents as well.

Shirley wasn't even properly awake when Sullivan called her at lunchtime and told her to get down to the Adelphi and start rehearsing, pronto. By the time Sullivan got to the theatre himself, the rehearsals had hit a serious obstacle; it seemed vital to Sullivan that Shirley should showcase 'Burn My Candle' in this new venue, since this was the highlight of her set – but they didn't have any sheet music for the song, and Ross Parker was out of town for the day. Sullivan immediately set about trying to track Parker down – and after a few phone calls eventually located him at a hotel in Brighton. He then got Parker to sing the melody line of the song over the phone to the Adelphi's orchestra leader Bill Ternant, so that Ternant could then score an arrangement for the musicians. The day was saved. Shirley's orchestra rehearsals lasted until the very last minute on that first night at the Adelphi; in fact, the theatre opened its doors a quarter of an hour late to accommodate her. When her slot in the revue came up, Shirley was introduced by the show's star, comedian Dave King, who failed to remember her name correctly.

It didn't matter. Once again, Shirley rose to the occasion and won the audience over from the start; most thought her performance the best part of the whole show. The Adelphi's publicist George Fearon had used Shirley's arrival in the show as an excuse to entice some new reviews from the half a dozen journalists he'd invited along to the theatre that night; afterwards, all of them wanted to talk to Shirley. She was repeatedly interviewed in her dressing room, and also posed for press photographs wearing a gold sheath dress that had been hastily unearthed from Jack Hylton's costume store. Shirley could only be photographed in the dress head on, as it had been hastily pinned up at the back to make it fit her.

The next morning, the national newspapers mentioned Shirley Bassey for the very first time. Michael Sullivan phoned her at noon to tell her the good news, but she just told him to go away, all she wanted to do was sleep; but when she finally saw the reviews, she was ecstatic, as she recalled in 1998: 'The press came on my first night and the next day they printed "The Tigress from Tiger Bay hits London", and I thought that was absolutely incredible. I thought, "They're talking about me! The Tigress from Tiger Bay!" I was always excited, and I hope that never leaves me.'

During her run at the Adelphi Theatre – where she was performing two shows a night – Shirley was also still playing at the Astor Club, although there were probably only a few days' overlap. Even so, it's a testament to her youthful stamina that she was able to carry this substantial workload without simply caving in; perhaps she should have done, because Sullivan now began to assume that Shirley could carry this kind of load indefinitely.

Some of the newspaper reports had touted Shirley as being 'Jack Hylton's newest discovery', and perhaps because of this Hylton quickly began pestering Sullivan for a share of his contract with Shirley. Sullivan stalled, partly because his contract with Shirley wasn't a watertight arrangement, and partly because he simply didn't want anyone else to have a share of the act he'd worked so hard to develop. Whichever way things should eventually turn out, Sullivan realised that he had to come to a more lasting agreement with Shirley. On the last night of her Adelphi run, he paid for Shirley's mother and sisters to come up from Cardiff to see the show, and afterwards they all posed for family photographs in Shirley's dressing room while she and Mike Sullivan signed a new five-year contract with each other. From now on, Shirley would receive a guaranteed £25 per week from Sullivan for the first year of the agreement (just over £1,000 in today's terms), and £60 a week for the second (roughly £2,600 today); after that, she would receive 5 per cent of all her income, with Mike Sullivan paying for her gowns, her publicity, her music, her pianists and all travel costs out of his own 45 per cent share.

After the Adelphi run, the standard fee Sullivan was receiving for Shirley's engagements went up to £60 a week (approximately £2,600 in today's terms), but Sullivan still had a lot of expenses – entertainment costs for all the journalists who now wanted to interview her, photographs to give away to all her new fans, and more – and according to him the Bassey business was still operating very much in the red.

During the period of the Sullivan-Hylton partnership, Shirley made at least one late-night TV broadcast from Hylton's Albany Club. Johnny Franz, an A&R man and record producer for Philips Records, happened to spot Shirley singing on the show and promptly got in touch with Sullivan to offer her a recording contract. When the two men met, Michael Sullivan was relieved that Franz agreed with his own assessment of his artist – which was that, despite her youth, Shirley should not be marketed as a teen idol for a teen audience and a flash-in-the-pan pop career. It would be far better to aim for an older market, and to build her audience slowly.

Shirley recorded 'Burn My Candle' (backed with 'Stormy Weather') as her first single some time during 1955 at the Philips recording studio in Bayswater, and it was released in February 1956. As previously mentioned, the powers that be at the BBC were shocked by the song's 'suggestive' lyrics ('who wants to help me burn my candle at both ends?'), and it was promptly banned from airplay. This was a serious setback, since the only alternative to the BBC in those days was Radio Luxembourg, which had terrible reception in Britain and was thus very annoying to listen to. Even so, the record still sold well, perhaps as a direct result of being banned.

For her first album, Johnny Franz cast Shirley in the role of a blues singer, much to her annoyance (though ironically, she's said in recent years that she would love to record a new album of blues and jazz material). But at the time – and for a long time into her career – she wasn't always happy with the choice of material that was made on her behalf. As she wrote in 1998: 'At the very beginning there was always somebody choosing my material and I didn't feel right with an awful lot of it. So when my manager used to tell me that I was going to be a big star one day, I thought in the back of my mind that if I ever became a star the first thing would be that nobody would choose material for me. I'd choose it, I decided.'

Meanwhile, although Jack Hylton was still effectively Michael

Sullivan's boss, he'd seemingly become resigned to the fact that he'd never own a share of Shirley's contract, and was magnanimous enough about it to agree to book Shirley into his next show at the Adelphi. This was another revue, *Such Is Life*, and it opened in mid-December for a 12-month run, its nominal star being the Northern comedian Al Read. However, Shirley Bassey was the act that virtually all the critics singled out for praise. One wrote, 'She sang her songs in a way that amounted to vocal arson. She was all electric and uninsulated. She is an 18-year-old coloured girl from the docks in Cardiff who hit rain-soaked London like a freak heat-wave'; another review ran, 'On the whole this is a show for the charabanc trade. Except that Miss Bassey, as she is in the limousine class.'

Plenty of men thought so too. Romantically, Shirley was playing the field, seeing a number of boyfriends on a casual basis for after-show suppers. Unfortunately for her, one of them became obsessively possessive, and violent to boot. One afternoon Shirley's dresser at the Adelphi, Helen Cooper, called Sullivan because she was concerned when Shirley showed up at the theatre with a bruised mouth. Sullivan arrived at the theatre to discover Shirley in her dressing room, putting on layers of make-up in an attempt to disguise her badly swollen lip and jaw; she also had a small cut on one arm. At first Shirley refused to tell Sullivan who had done this to her, but eventually she told him the whole story. It seemed that one of the boys she'd been dating hadn't taken the hint when she'd stood him up on several occasions. He'd threatened her and warned her not to go out with other men, but she'd ignored him. Then, the previous night, he'd followed her home after a date, had pushed his way inside her room and punched her squarely in the face.

According to Sullivan, Shirley then begged him to 'Do something, please do something. I never thought it would get like this.' The manager took prompt action, confronting the boy's mother about the matter; she turned out to be an ally, since she actively disapproved of her son seeing Shirley romantically, and promised that she would keep her son in line. In return, Sullivan agreed not to press charges (which would only have resulted in bad publicity for Shirley), but he did insist on arranging for a friendly police detective from Bow Street to have a quiet word with the boy and warn him off. Sullivan doesn't name Shirley's assailant in his autobiography; according to Muriel Burgess, he was 19-year-old Terence Clyde Davies, nicknamed 'Pepe', and he was to prove an ongoing problem. Within two months, Shirley was dating him regularly once again.

Even though he disapproved, Sullivan couldn't prevent Shirley from continuing the relationship, so he did his best to wear her out by keeping her so busy that she wouldn't have time to see her beau. Apart from her live shows, Shirley was now making regular TV appearances, taking part in a weekly radio show, attending recording sessions, press interviews and photo sessions, as well as undertaking extra publicity work, such as appearing at dress shop openings (where she usually received a free dress or two as a perk). If all this weren't enough, in early 1956 Sullivan also found her an extra job, appearing in nightly cabaret at the Embassy Club in Bond Street. She was still performing two shows a night at the Adelphi; two hours after coming offstage there she was standing behind a microphone at the Embassy.

But although Shirley had – briefly – managed to cope with this kind of schedule before, there were still limits even to her endurance, and this pace soon began to take its toll. One night she nearly fainted while coming offstage at the Adelphi, and was proud of the fact that she'd managed to disguise it, so that the audience didn't notice. Sullivan's response when she told him about this was to express disappointment that her fainting fit hadn't happened while she was centre stage, since it would have generated a lot of newspaper coverage. Shirley was not amused.

Another night Shirley had a physical fight with the stage director at the Adelphi; it began as a screaming match over her lateness in arriving on stage, and then he slapped her face and she slapped him right back again. Michael Sullivan arrived on the scene, having come to collect Shirley to take her to film another TV show at the Albany Club, and attempted to calm her down, but she insisted that she was ill, and couldn't possibly do the TV show now; when he tried to reason with her, she started throwing pots of make-up at him. 'The more I tried to calm her down, the more hysterical she became,' he later recalled. Shirley was now crying and screaming, and Sullivan could think of nothing else to do but to slap her again – which served merely to make her hysteria worse. Eventually, the theatre manager Bill Porter intervened in the situation, and managed to pacify Shirley enough for Sullivan to be able to bundle her into a taxi.

Shirley apparently thought she was being driven home, so when the taxi pulled up at the Albany she went into a rage again, accusing Sullivan of having conned her. Entering the club, Sullivan quickly pushed Shirley into the ladies' toilet, and attempted to calm her down again, to little avail. Hearing all the noise, another act on the bill – impressionist Eddie Arnold – brushed Sullivan aside, insisting that he could sort things out. Arnold then gave Shirley a powerful slap on the face – the third one she had received that evening, and it did nothing to improve her mood. 'At this rate I was going to end up with a punch-drunk singer,' recalled Sullivan.

Events were finally resolved when Jack Hylton arrived to investigate all the commotion. 'What are you doing with this girl?' he demanded of Sullivan. According to Sullivan, Hylton then gave Shirley a tranquillizer pill, led her away and comforted her. Whether because of the tranquillizer or not, Shirley was somehow able to perform before the cameras that night after all, and after performing she sat at Hylton's table, quietly sipping champagne. When Sullivan neared the table, Hylton told him, 'Get away from her. You've done enough.' Knowing it to be for the best, Sullivan did as he was told, though as he was leaving he thought he detected a glint of triumph in Shirley's gaze.

To give him his due, Sullivan at least realized that all this had come to a head because he'd been badly overworking Shirley, and he claimed that in the week following the Albany incident he cancelled as many of her future commitments as he could. After Shirley's Embassy run was over the pace did begin to ease a little, but even so she continued to take other professional engagements on top of her Adelphi work – and not all of them went smoothly. Booked to perform at the Savoy Social Club at Rushey Green, Shirley discovered that she was expected to sing with an unknown band, without any rehearsal at all. The band weren't even able to play Shirley's written song arrangements; somehow she managed to perform three numbers that they all knew before finally admitting defeat. Having sung for only half the agreed time, she was paid half the agreed fee. Another singing engagement, held at the Dorchester Hotel, was the annual dinner for the employees (and their wives) of a boiler-making firm from Wolverhampton. The company was so large that the event took place over two nights, a week apart. This time the audience liked the sexy young singer in the tight dress only too much – or rather, the male half did, which immediately drew the disapproval and hostility of their wives and girlfriends. Shirley's applause began to diminish after her second number, as the men became aware that they were being subjected to evil glares from their partners. Shirley was mystified as to what could possibly have gone wrong, until Sullivan explained that the women in the audience were less than happy with her. Confirmation came a few days later when a letter arrived from the company's entertainments committee explaining that Shirley had somehow upset the wives. As a result, she was asked not to sing at the second night of the dinner, although she was still paid in full for both.

*

According to Muriel Burgess, in spring 1956 Shirley acquired a new love interest in Bernard Hall, nicknamed 'Balls', whom she met in Olivelli's restaurant. Hall, aged 27, was a dancer who was originally from London, but who now resided in Monte Carlo; he was in town to recruit other dancers for a performance at the forthcoming wedding celebrations of Prince Rainier and Grace Kelly. Hall and Shirley conducted a month-long love affair, until he left town again – although they would remain friends, and occasionally lovers, for many years to come.

Shirley was now spending a small fortune on clothes and shoes, which slightly concerned Sullivan. He came to the conclusion that if she was going to act as if she was a star already, then he'd better make her one, and quickly. The ideal showcase for Shirley, he thought, would be an appearance at the Café de Paris, situated between Piccadilly Circus and Leicester Square, a lavish nightclub which only booked the top cabaret acts in the world, such as Noël Coward, Marlene Dietrich and Eartha Kitt. Sullivan accordingly approached the venue's owner, Major Donald Neville-Whiting, and begged him to give Shirley a chance. Neville-Whiting, a dapper little man (Sullivan calls him 'elfin') who sported a monocle, knew all there was to know about show business, having run ENSA shows during the war, and he operated at the very top of the game.

Sullivan promised Neville-Whiting that if he gave Shirley an opening, he would spend her entire fee for the engagement on publicity and new costumes – whatever it took to make her appearance at the club a roaring success. The Major gave Sullivan a series of polite brush-offs, but the manager still persisted. Eventually, in June 1956 Sullivan received a call from Neville-Whiting asking if Shirley was free to perform at the Café de Paris during the first two weeks of September, since an act had fallen through and the club now had a vacancy for those dates; needless to say, Sullivan immediately agreed. In the event, Shirley's opening at the Café was delayed for several weeks until the end of September because Liberace – a huge star at the time – suddenly became available to play there then.

A couple of months still wasn't much time to prepare Shirley for the highest-profile event of her career to date – and there was another problem to be dealt with first of all. Sullivan's relationship with Jack Hylton was by now on its last legs, and would come to a complete end within two months. Under the terms of Shirley's contract with Jack Hylton, he had the right to veto any of her other appearances for the duration of her Adelphi run. Hylton had never exercised this veto before, but he did so now, perhaps because of his deteriorating alliance with Sullivan. The only way Sullivan could get him to relent was by agreeing to pay him £200 (nearly £9,000 in today's terms). This was half of Shirley's entire fee for the two-week run at the Café, but Sullivan thought it well worthwhile if it bought her a chance for real stardom.

For the Café de Paris shows Sullivan engaged the services of songwriter Ian Grant (who had written songs for Jack Buchanan and for West End revues), pianist Les Paul (former accompanist for Gracie Fields, and not to be confused with the famous guitarist) and musical arranger Bill Oliver, who would oversee the club's house band. Sullivan also had a new black gown designed for Shirley to wear, with mink trim around the bustline.

As a publicity gimmick, Sullivan and Neville-Whiting agreed between them that admittance to Shirley's opening night should be by invitation only, with the audience consisting only of the aristocracy, the very wealthy and A-list celebrities. Evening dress was compulsory. When Shirley was informed that it was likely that she might be asked to join some of the nobility at one of their tables after her show, she went into panic mode – largely because she was terrified that she might use the wrong knife and fork. Sullivan accordingly took her for a meal at a very expensive restaurant and gave her a crash course in genteel table manners and cutlery identification.

As the opening night drew closer, Shirley got increasingly more nervous. The dress rehearsal the night before the opening went badly, and Shirley was in tears afterwards. Sullivan insisted that she went straight home and got an early night. The next morning Sullivan received a call from Papa Olivelli, the owner of the restaurant above which Shirley was living, to say that Shirley was in tears, and to come quickly. When Sullivan arrived at Shirley's flat, he tried to bolster her confidence, telling her not to worry, that she was sure to triumph that night – but to his amazement Shirley revealed that she wasn't crying about the show at all, but about something else entirely.

The previous evening she had gone to the cinema with Barry Hamilton, a young singer who also lived above Olivelli's. Afterwards there had been another scene with the obsessively jealous 'Pepe' Davies, who had followed her home once again. Shirley told him that this was the last straw, and that their relationship was over for good. Davies promptly stormed out of her flat, and shortly afterwards there was an appalling noise outside in the street; Davies had crashed his car into the gates of a garage immediately opposite Shirley's flat. She found him lying on the pavement, his face covered in blood. Shirley had wanted to go to the hospital with him, but Hamilton and other friends refused to let her go, knowing how important the following night was for her career. She had rung the hospital that morning, and Davies was still on the danger list.

Sullivan refused to let Shirley go to the hospital, and told her that she should let Davies drop out of her life for good; whether this had been a suicide attempt or not, Davies had his own family to look after him, and the best thing Shirley could do now was to

71

forget him. Sullivan then arranged for his wife Juhni to stay with Shirley for the rest of the day, until she went on stage at the Adelphi that night. The Adelphi shows went well, and Shirley's nerves began to subside slightly when she arrived at the Café de Paris to discover her dressing room filled with flowers and congratulatory telegrams (most of which had actually been sent by Sullivan). Shirley's mother had made the trip from Cardiff to see her daughter sing that night decked out in diamond earrings, bracelet and neck-lace – £10,000 worth of jewellery which Sullivan had hired for the occasion (and worth about £450,000 today).

Once again, Shirley triumphed, and the applause was deafening; among the celebrity-studded audience that night were Liberace and his brother George. Ian Grant had written two numbers for Shirley's set at Sullivan's request, the titles of which demonstrate the image that the manager still wanted his singer to convey: 'My Body's More Important Than My Mind' and 'Sex.' Although these two songs were undoubtedly risqué material at the time and prob-ably gave the audience a brief frisson of naughtiness, neither song was particularly striking either musically or lyrically, or had any lasting existence after the Café de Paris run was over (although a live EP of the show was released shortly afterwards, which would re-surface on CD in 2008). In the post-show confusion that first night, Sullivan forgot to collect the jewellery from Shirley and return it. Not knowing what to do for the best, Shirley and her mother had returned to the flat above Olivelli's, terrified that they were going to be robbed at any moment on their way home. Once inside, Shirley locked the door and windows, and slept with the diamonds under her pillow. When Sullivan showed up the next morning, she couldn't give the gems back to him quickly enough, adamant that he should never hire jewellery for her ever again.

Shirley's run at the Café de Paris was a roaring success, and was soon extended from two weeks to nine; in the course of this time she became very close to Major Donald Neville-Whiting, who treated her like his own daughter. Shirley confided her fears to the Major about Mike Sullivan, whom she still believed was treating her unfairly financially. When Neville-Whiting confronted Sullivan about this, the manager happily outlined all his income and expenses, and proved to the Major's satisfaction that he was actually making a £400 loss on the nine-week run.

But it was money well spent. As well as receiving coverage in all the Fleet Street newspapers, Shirley was now getting photo features in glossy society magazines like *The Sketch* and *Tatler* as well; in November she made the front cover of the prestigious *Picture Post* magazine, as 'The Girl From Tiger Bay' was profiled by the noted journalist Katharine Whitehorn. As a result of all this, Sullivan now began to receive offers of work from overseas for Shirley after her Adelphi contract came to an end in December. In short, that year Michael Sullivan had succeeded in all of his ambitions for Shirley. She was now truly established as a star in Britain, and it was time to introduce her to the rest of the world.

f i v e

THE WORLD

The first time Shirley Bassey ever left England, in late December 1956, it was to perform as part of a radio show broadcast from the Olympia Theatre in Paris. When they arrived in the city Michael Sullivan was in a generous mood, and he gave Shirley the entire £100 fee for the show, so that she could indulge herself in a Parisian shopping spree. Quite a spree, since this would be equivalent to over £4,000 today.

Unfortunately, Shirley's pianist Les Paul was still stuck in Britain, having been stranded by severe fog at London airport. There was no way that Paul would be able get to Paris by boat-train in time for the show – and he still had all the sheet music of Shirley's orchestral arrangements with him. Fortunately, the 26-piece orchestra at the Olympia were true professionals, and they rose to the occasion. Shirley only had to perform two songs, and both of them were standards – 'Stormy Weather' and 'I Can't Give You Anything But Love.' After a brief rehearsal, Shirley and the musicians gelled, and the broadcast performance went extremely well. So much so, in fact, that the Olympia immediately offered Shirley a month-long booking, at £350 per week (over £15,000 in today's terms).

Meanwhile, Sammy Lewis, the entertainments manager for the

New Frontier Hotel in Las Vegas, had seen Shirley singing at the Café de Paris, and wanted to book her to fill a two-week vacancy at the New Frontier at the end of January 1957. In those days Las Vegas was nowhere near as glamorous as it would soon become, and consisted of only a handful of hotels and casinos, but even so, it was an important foothold for any artist hoping to break into the USA. Having agreed terms with Lewis, Sullivan recruited Harold Foster of the William Morris agency to try and line up some more work in the country for Shirley, and Foster came up with a number of extra dates, including a booking at Ciro's in Hollywood. Then, a week before Shirley was due to arrive in Las Vegas, the New Frontier Hotel went into liquidation, and her deal there suddenly no longer existed. Fortunately, Foster was soon able to come up with a replacement booking in Vegas for her that was even better, at the more established El Rancho.

According to Sullivan, all of the attention that Shirley was now getting went to her head, and she wanted the trappings of stardom she now felt were her due – specifically, a mink coat and a white Jaguar sports car. At the same time, Sullivan was wondering how he would ever be able to afford their air fares to the USA. In the end, he had to borrow the fares – and £200 'mad money' – from his accountant. Sullivan always seemed to spend more than he earned, which was never enough. En route to Nevada, Sullivan even had to do some fast footwork to avoid the policemen who were waiting at London airport with a warrant for his arrest; this was because of unpaid alimony that he owed to his second wife. In fact, Sullivan had just split up from his third wife, Juhni, and was now taking his new love, a Greek dancer named Lily Berde, to the USA with him.

When their plane landed in New York, Shirley was kept waiting at immigration control until long after Sullivan, Lily and all the other white passengers had all been processed through. It was her first taste of the different racial attitudes prevailing in the USA, where segregation was still rife in the Southern states and the civil rights movement had barely even begun. Though she had encountered discrimination at home in Britain – both at school and from boarding house landladies in her touring days –Shirley had never taken it that seriously, or that personally. 'I had a white mother and I'd been brought up in an all-white area, so colour wasn't a big issue for me until I went to America and found out what black Americans were going through,' she later commented. She'd see far more of this on later trips, but this time too there were incidents; when they got to Las Vegas, Sullivan was quietly warned that he shouldn't be seen dining in public with Shirley too often, lest people think they were actually dating. Even in the lavish surroundings of Vegas, Sullivan ran the risk of being beaten up if he was seen publicly breaking racial taboos.

*

Although they were in New York for only five days, when Sullivan visited the offices of Columbia Records (who represented Philips Records in the USA), he somehow managed to arrange a New York recording date for Shirley, to take place just a few days later. The session was to be produced by Mitch Miller, at that time one of the top record producers in the world, who had worked with Frank Sinatra, Johnnie Ray and many others.

If Shirley was impressed, she didn't show it. Her sudden success was going to her 20-year-old head, and Sullivan was finding her harder and harder to handle. As he recalled in his autobiography:

> Shirley had no idea of the work I had put in, the long hours of bargaining, the stunts I had pulled to bring her along so fast. True, she had the voice and the stage personality to make it all worth doing, but I had been the one who had done it. The idea was just entertaining Shirley's mind that she was a major star and that I worked for her – although it was to be some time before she actually put this thought into words. Her new fame was bringing her into continual contact with important and rich people, and I did not dare let her know how my finances stood, that the gamble was still on and far from over.

In New York, Sullivan hired publicity agent Ed Gollin to squire Shirley around Manhattan and introduce her to some of those 'important and rich people.' Gollin took Shirley to see the Broadway musical *Mr Wonderful*, starring Sammy Davis Jr. After the show they went backstage, where Davis told Shirley how flattered he had been when she had sung his praises in her interview with the African-American magazine *Ebony*. He took Shirley to dinner, and then on to see Frank Sinatra perform at the Copacabana; after Sinatra's set Shirley and Sammy joined the singer at his table, but Frank was in an unsociable mood that night and didn't even talk to them. Shirley was also pestered by the Copacabana's owner Joe Padella, who wanted her to sing at his club. When she explained that she had contracts elsewhere and so could not oblige, Padella became angry; even if he was only play-acting, Shirley found

Padella a terrifying, gangster-like figure, so what should have been a thrilling evening became an ordeal, and she fled the scene as soon as she could. She would meet Sinatra again, though, and within a few years rumours of an affair between the two of them began to circulate, which both parties strenuously denied.

Shirley's recording session with Mitch Miller came at the end of their stay in New York, and was, according to Sullivan, 'a disaster.' In readiness for the session Shirley should have memorized the lyrics to the two songs they were due to record, but she had been far too occupied with nightclubbing and watching late-night TV to pay them any mind; and to make matters worse, she had also cancelled the two rehearsal sessions with a pianist that had been arranged for her. As Miller was a perfectionist, when it became apparent that she just couldn't get the phrasing of one song right, he threatened to cancel the whole session.

Sullivan talked him round, and somehow they all muddled through it, with Shirley later complaining that she'd been given nowhere near the amount of support and rehearsal she was used to receiving from her English producer Johnny Franz; Sullivan told her she had got off lightly, and was lucky not to have received a spanking. Despite the problems, the session still managed to result in a single: 'If I Had a Needle and Thread' backed with 'Tonight My Heart She Is Crying.'

Leaving New York, Shirley, Sullivan and Lily flew on to Las Vegas. When they arrived at the El Rancho, Shirley was allocated a wooden cabin in the hotel grounds, and Sullivan and Lily were given another. The next day, Sullivan and Lily moved to a cheaper motel nearby, in an attempt at budgeting; financially, Sullivan was still scraping by on a wing and a prayer while trying to save enough cash to pay for their air fares to California. Things began to improve as soon as Shirley started performing (and thus earning money) again, since the hotel was paying her $1,800 a week (approximately £25,000 in today's terms), although 10% went to the William Morris agency straight away; of the remaining $1,620, Shirley was given $350 a week, out of which she was supposed to pay her own hotel bill (of $98).

Performing at the El Rancho took a little getting used to for Shirley, since drinks and meals were still being served to the audience during the performance, which was standard procedure in American nightclubs in those days. Shirley had to learn to sing louder than usual in order to combat the background clatter of knives, forks and plates – and the never-ending sound of people feeding coins into one-armed bandits in the distance. Shirley's first show finished at 9.40 p.m., and she wasn't on stage again till one in the morning – in the hours in between, she herself hit the one-armed bandits with a vengeance, almost always losing. It was a bad habit that would give Sullivan a nasty shock a few weeks later.

Because the venue was so totally different from anything Sullivan had ever encountered in England, he found it impossible to judge whether Shirley's Las Vegas debut had been a success or not – but was relieved when the verdict of the critics was uniformly ecstatic. One local paper's review ran, 'She is unbelievable, her voice is sensational, her delivery is strong and she is charm itself to look at.' Sullivan sent out copies of these reviews to 2,000 US newspapers and magazines; an expensive business in those pre-photostat days, but it paid off, with 800 of those papers running further news items plugging Shirley to the American market.

A few weeks into their stay in Vegas, Shirley insisted that Sullivan accompany her one afternoon to a room in the Dunes Hotel, where two very pleasant gentlemen gave him a drink and then showed him the mink stole that Shirley had picked out for herself earlier that day. The cost was a mere $15,000, including insurance (something like £200,000 in today's money). Sullivan had to take Shirley aside and gently point out that he couldn't buy it for her – as his money was needed for other expenses – and that at the moment she simply couldn't afford to buy it for herself, either. Shirley accepted the situation with good grace, and admitted that she'd been silly to think she could buy such a luxury item.

But when Sullivan got back to his motel, he immediately phoned the fur salesman at the Dunes. 'Perversely, I now wanted Shirley to have it because she had behaved so well when I told her that she couldn't,' he recorded. So Sullivan and the salesman struck a deal for the mink. Sullivan would pay $11,000 for the stole, $300 down and $100 per week until the balance was paid off. He'd pay the deposit himself, and the weekly payments would thereafter be made by Shirley. One hour later, Sullivan presented the delighted Shirley with her mink stole, and the news that she'd be paying for it herself in instalments didn't diminish her joy one iota.

Shirley's stint at the El Rancho went down so well that the hotel immediately re-booked her to return for future engagements over the next two years; she'd get $3,000 a week for the first season, and $5,000 a week in the second year (not at all a bad offer, since the very top dollar for cabaret artists at this time was $8,000 a week). In the event, Shirley was never able to take advantage of this deal, as the unfortunate El Rancho burned down before she could return.

The trio then moved on to Los Angeles, where Shirley was due to play at Ciro's nightclub on Sunset Strip for the next six weeks, at $2,000 per week (of which the William Morris agency took 10 per cent). The sum would today be equivalent to roughly £29,000. Shirley told Sullivan that she wanted to stay somewhere in LA that had its own swimming pool, and he tried his best to oblige her. The first half dozen hotels he tried were either far too expensive, or completely booked up – or else simply claiming that they were, having been first informed by Sullivan that 'Miss Bassey is coloured'. Even liberal California was not exempt from racism in those days. Eventually, Sullivan found Shirley an apartment in a block that had its own bar and pool. It cost $10 a day (roughly £120 in today's money), and Sullivan and Lily booked (separately) into cheaper motels nearby. The first night in LA, Sullivan decided to take them all to Ciro's for dinner, so that they could see for themselves what the place was like; Shirley was due to open there in three days time.

The building's exterior seemed promising, with its huge, illuminated letter 'C'; there were also two uniformed doormen and a parking attendant. Unfortunately, although the club had once been a haven for Hollywood stars, its heyday had been a good 10 years earlier; and although the club would later have a resurgence as a rock venue during the hippie era, it was currently in a slump. Inside, Ciro's 'was a dreary room with cheap décor, and business was terrible.' That night the successful American comedienne Frances Faye was playing to a house of only 30 or so people, and Sullivan began to fear that the unknown Shirley could only hope for the worst possible reception there.

He need not have worried – the house band, he discovered, was

good, and when Shirley opened that weekend, things went well, as
Sullivan later recounted:

> Shirley with her big occasion temperament was at her most electri-
> fying at the opening. She put the audience into a state of shock and
> they stopped eating and drinking, which is something at an American
> club. The newspapers labelled her 'the girl who livened up the strip'
> and Ciro's did better business than it had before she arrived.

Things were beginning to look up, until Sullivan got a phonecall
from Las Vegas a few days later. Unfortunately, although Shirley
had paid her hotel bill at the El Rancho in full, all the coins she had
drawn from the hotel's receptionist to lose in slot machines had
been put on a *separate* bill, and Sullivan was now being asked to pay
up. The total came to over $600 (equivalent to about £8,500
today). Sullivan told them to send the bill to the William Morris
agency, with whom he'd sort things out later (the agency grudgingly obliged), and gave Shirley a stiff lecture about watching out
for hidden extras on hotel bills.

But the bill was just the start of their Californian problems. When
Sullivan went to collect the salary for Shirley's first week from Ciro's
manager Herman Hover, he was given a mere $300 on account, and
asked to wait a few days for the balance. Ciro's paid William Morris
their $200 directly, which left $1,500 due to Sullivan – and he'd been
counting on the money badly. He gave $250 to Shirley, which left
him with only $50 to his name. Sullivan had his motel bill to pay,
and Shirley was supposed to pay an instalment on her mink stole.
Sullivan had also been asked to pay a week's rent in advance on his

room, but had put the motel management off with promises of the money he'd be receiving from Ciro's; now he had to ask them for further time to pay, and they weren't very happy about it. For the next three days Sullivan chased Hover, trying to get the money out of him, but the manager kept making excuses. Then Sullivan came home one night to discover that he'd been locked out of his motel room, and that all his belongings had been put under lock and key as collateral (the motel wouldn't even let him unpack a toothbrush for himself). He slept that night in the back seat of his car, and in the morning drove to Lily's motel and explained his problems; she lent him the money to pay his bill (and redeem his luggage), and he then moved into a room at her motel, where the management were more sympathetic and he had Lily to vouch for him.

The Ciro's money slowly filtered through in dribs and drabs, just enough so that Sullivan was able to pay everybody he needed to (including the mink salesmen) and survive – although he had the occasional near-penniless day of living on coffee and doughnuts. Sullivan kept his misfortunes from Shirley, who was keeping herself busy during the day by learning to drive on the streets of Hollywood. She failed her driving test by driving through a red light, but then bought herself a provisional licence for $30 which enabled her to keep on driving regardless (though Sullivan doubtless thought about how many doughnuts he could buy for that amount).

One night Sullivan was unable to get to Ciro's at all, and the next day Shirley told him that she'd been approached in his absence by a group of four men who wanted to buy her management contract, and who'd promised they could greatly increase her fees for engagements, especially in Las Vegas. 'I don't mind if you do a deal with them where you stay in, too,' Shirley told him, a sign that – Sullivan felt – she still regarded him as just a 'labourer.' Sullivan met with the men at Ciro's that night. They boasted of their connections in Vegas, and made veiled allusions as to their working methods. 'It was clear that these four were hoodlums, and trying to make me believe that they were very big-time hoodlums at that,' Sullivan concluded. He refused to let the men intimidate him, and told them that he would be happy to sell them a 50 per cent share in his management contract with Shirley, for the sum of $75,000 – roughly half a million pounds in today's terms. But Sullivan would only make this deal if it were negotiated through the lawyers of the William Morris agency. Since the Vegas gentlemen were evidently not keen on dealing with the law in any form, that was the last that Sullivan and Shirley ever heard from them.

Still, Sullivan was happier when they eventually left town, and didn't even seem to mind the fact that Ciro's still owed them money. The Morris agency had booked Shirley next into the Riverside Room in Reno, Nevada, at $1,500 a week (roughly £500 at the time, equivalent to about £21,000 today). She and Sullivan had a good time in Reno, perhaps because things were less fraught financially – although Shirley really worried her manager one night by staying out all night. She worried him even more the next day by telling him that she'd run off to elope. That had been her plan, anyway, although fortunately it had all come to nothing. 'After the show I met this really good-looking man and we had some drinks and the subject of marriage came up,' she told Sullivan. 'He proposed and I got terribly romantic about it. I thought it was marvellous, being proposed to, and I also thought that, being in Reno, I could get a quickie divorce before I leave, so I accepted. We went in his car and drove all over the place, talking about the wedding, for hours. He even got a friend of his with a radio station to congratulate us over the air, but there was no mention of a wedding. Then it got light and I thought, "Bit weird. He's got no intention of marrying me." All he wanted to do was take me home and get me into bed. What he did do was waste the whole night talking. Why couldn't he have just come out with it instead?'

According to Sullivan, Shirley received two further marriage proposals while she was in Reno – both of them from midgets. One evening in the hotel lobby Shirley saw a group of small men at the reception desk, and learned that they were in town for a midgets' convention. Shirley became suddenly concerned that they might take offence at one of the songs in her set, a reworking of Cole Porter's 'Let's Do It' which included the line: 'even little men who have to reach do it.' She sought a second opinion from a Moroccan acrobat, who was one of the other acts on the bill. He told her that the best way to handle the situation was to not to change the lyrics at all but – if there were any midgets in the audience – to look them straight in the eyes and smile while she sang, thus including them in the joke rather than making them the butt of it. Shirley followed this advice, and when she got to the line in question, she looked directly at the group of little men in the audience and smiled – and, as one, they all roared with laughter. After this incident two of the midgets followed Shirley everywhere she went in the hotel, each of them separately trying to persuade her to marry him.

*

In February 1957, a week before she flew back to Britain, Sullivan learned that Shirley had just scored her first real chart hit back home, with her version of the calypso 'Banana Boat Song.' Shirley hadn't wanted to record the song in the first place, but Johnny Franz had talked her into it; now Franz's judgement was paying off, and there would soon be some much-needed cash in the Bassey/ Sullivan coffers. The record eventually reached number eight in the charts, but Shirley's version of the song was soon overtaken by Harry Belafonte's (her version was a lot sexier). According to Muriel Burgess, Shirley had first performed the song live at the Adelphi in 1955, wearing a multi-coloured turban with plumes. The 'Banana Boat Song' would also (much later) become a regular staple of the Kinks' stage act.

Meanwhile, Sullivan was desperately trying to raise the money for their air fare home to Britain. Knowing that Shirley had a hit record, he moved fast, and struck a deal with the promoter Leslie Grade for Shirley to appear in one of his touring variety shows. Sullivan got everything he asked for in the deal, including two airline tickets home from Reno.

*

Back in London, Shirley booked into the Mayfair Hotel. Her room cost the then incredible price of £60 per week, but Sullivan's idea was to place her in plush surroundings for press interviews and meetings with agents and bookers. However, this was a bill that Shirley had to pay herself, and as soon as she possibly could, she booked herself out again. There was no way that she would contemplate moving back to Olivelli's, but Sullivan was completely taken aback when she told him where she planned to stay in London next. She'd accepted an invitation from Pepe Davies's mother, and had moved into the Davies family home, where she shared a room with Pepe's sister Gloria. Pepe had been ill for a long time following his accident, but was now completely recovered, and Shirley felt sure there would be no more romantic problems with him; almost anybody could have predicted there would be, since Shirley was dating other men while she was living there, but fortunately, she wasn't there very much at all in the short term, as the Grade variety tour kicked off almost immediately.

Three weeks into the tour Shirley was due to play in Cardiff, and Sullivan concocted elaborate plans to turn her homecoming into a huge publicity stunt. Sullivan had a penchant for these, but they failed as often as they worked; when they flew in from Reno he'd arranged for Shirley to be presented at London airport with a model boat full of bananas, certain that photographs of this would make all the newspapers. In the event, not a single newspaper published a picture. For the Cardiff date, Sullivan had arranged for Shirley's train to be met at Cardiff station by the local Boy Scouts, Girl Guides and Boys Brigades (and their marching bands), as well as by 140 teenagers from the Rainbow Club that Shirley had once belonged to (Sullivan having made a sizeable donation to the club on Shirley's behalf). Her train was to be decked out in a banner that read 'WELCOME HOME SHIRLEY BASSEY', and she was to ride the short distance from the station to her hotel in an open-topped limousine. A few days before Shirley's arrival, however, the Cardiff police got wind of Sullivan's planned 'parade', and informed him that they simply wouldn't allow it. Sullivan refused to cancel his plans, and was told that he would be arrested if the event went ahead. 'This is the first time Cardiff has produced an international

star,' he told the police, and dared them to arrest both himself and
Shirley on the day; the publicity if they did so would be enormous,
and Cardiff would come out of the situation a lot worse off than
Shirley Bassey.

When Shirley's train pulled into Cardiff station, the platform
was absolutely jammed with people, and her rapturous welcome
went off without a hitch. There was no sign of the police at all. In
addition to all the teenagers that Sullivan had drafted in, the route
to Shirley's hotel half a mile away was lined with another 600
people who had simply turned up. 'Shirley cried, accepted two
bouquets that I had paid for and sat on the back seat of the limousine waving the way she had seen American presidents do,' Sullivan
recalled. The following night Shirley opened at Cardiff's New
Theatre to a packed house; the day after she received a heroine's
welcome when she visited the Rainbow Club.

There were also family issues to be discussed while she was in
Cardiff. Shirley's daughter Sharon had been raised for most of her
life by Shirley's sister Iris and her husband Bill, who now wanted
to adopt the little girl and make the arrangement a permanent
one. Shirley had agreed to this in principle ages before, but every
time she actually saw her daughter in the flesh, she wavered and
postponed signing the necessary legal papers. Sharon was now
walking and talking, and was very confused about Shirley's role in
her life: if she saw Shirley in a photograph she would refer to her
as 'mummy', but when they met in person she would call her
'Auntie Shirley', and 'mummy' very definitely meant Iris and no
one else. Shirley now realized she should let the adoption proceed,
but it wasn't an easy decision for her. As she said in 1998: 'Children

have to have a home and mothers should be at home looking after them. I wasn't working so much then, but my destiny was to sing and I found it very difficult and heartbreaking to leave [her]. It really was.' On another occasion, Shirley asked the pragmatically rhetorical question: 'At 17, what could I have offered her?'

*

Shirley's finances were nearly always the cause of her arguments with Sullivan, since she now wanted all the trappings of stardom possessed by other stars (usually ones who were far more successful than she was). Even though he was only contractually obligated to pay Shirley £65 a week, after talks with his accountant Sullivan increased her wage to £125 per week (equivalent to just over £5,000 today). He wanted her to be happy with their relationship, after all. Sullivan also made all the arrangements when Shirley announced that she wanted to buy her mother a house in Cardiff. It cost £4,000 (about £165,000 in modern terms, possibly much more), but Shirley wanted to pay for it quickly, so Sullivan organised matters so that large deductions would be made from Shirley's earnings, which only led to further squabbles about money in the future.

As she stated in 2003, Shirley felt that she owed her mother almost everything, for Eliza had supported her career from the start: 'I think she felt she'd made a mess of her own life, so she was especially thrilled that one of her children was making something of hers. In the end, I was able to spoil her. I bought her a house and clothes and her own fur coat, which she cherished.' In fact, the house in question – on the Newport Road, far away from Splott and the Bay, in a much nicer neighbourhood – was the first of three houses that Shirley would eventually buy for her mother, the last being a luxury bungalow. Eliza was now a widow twice over; not only had Mr Mendi recently passed away, but she had received word from Nigeria several years earlier that Henry Bassey was now dead.

As for Shirley, she made another brief foray abroad to play dates in Stockholm and Belgium. She also went to Monte Carlo for the first time, where she sang at a gala affair at the Sporting Club but absolutely bombed (the customers were far more interested in dining, flirting with each other and gambling); Sullivan cushioned the blow by telling her that the applause had been inaudible to her because of bad acoustics. After the gala she played a week's residency at Monte Carlo's Sea Club where, by contrast, she went over a storm. During that week Shirley took up with a boy named Nicky, the son of a Greek shipping magnate, and spent most of her spare time on his yacht. The couple were inseparable for a week, but afterwards never saw each other again.

July saw her topping the variety bill for the first time in London, during a two-week run at the Hippodrome. Shirley and Sullivan argued (again) about what costume she should wear for this prestigious engagement. He'd had a gold lamé dress with a halter neck made for her, which was slit at the front almost to the waist. Shirley had other ideas, and proudly modelled the dress she herself had designed and wanted to wear. It was white crinoline with a diamanté top, and Sullivan's verdict of it was that Shirley looked like 'the first black Cinderella I've ever seen.' Needless to say, Sullivan won the day, and Shirley dutifully wore the gold lamé creation on stage. Sullivan paid David Jacobs, then Britain's top disc jockey, to introduce Shirley every night, and at the end of each performance 16 bouquets of flowers were presented to her on stage, all of them paid for by Michael Sullivan. Pete Townshend of The Who saw Shirley singing live around this period (when he was 12) and recalled 50 years later that the young star from Cardiff 'blew the roof off. She could only have been in her teens. She wore a dress that clung to her body as closely as a seaweed wrap. Her voice soared above the band and she hardly used the microphone provided.'

Shirley was billed in the Hippodrome's programme as 'Britain's Sepia Songstress.' Though the phrase makes one wince today, it was just an example of the unthinking mindset of the times, and almost certainly no offence was intended. That's not to say that racism didn't exist then, or that Shirley didn't encounter it; some of the letters that arrived among her fan mail were openly hateful. 'They asked me why I didn't go back to where I came from,' Shirley would recall decades later. 'I was always tempted to write back and say, "What, Splott"?'

Towards the end of the Hippodrome run Sullivan became ill with pleural pneumonia, but refused to go to hospital and continued working from his bed. Shirley didn't make life any easier for him, either, as he recounted in his autobiography:

> She was 20 years old, she was reading the posters I had written which said she was a fabulous star and she was living the part in the way she saw it. Getting her to rehearse a new song was like leading a reluctant schoolgirl to her lessons. She was temperamental with theatre musical directors and one day she cost Philips Records a lot

of money by going to her hairdresser instead of keeping a recording date and leaving 40 musicians cooling their heels in the studio. On another occasion she walked out of a BBC TV *Six-Five Special* show because she was told she could not keep her dog, a white miniature poodle called Beaujolais, in her dressing room. She went back later, but not until the producer, the director and the band had passed a panic-filled three hours.

During this period there was also the occasion when Shirley and some friends ended up having a physical fight with a nightclub owner over a dinner bill that she refused to pay; Sullivan quietly settled the account the next day, but Shirley was starting to upset far too many people, and it couldn't go on.

*

While Shirley was away on tour, an X-ray revealed that Sullivan was now suffering from tuberculosis. Hospitalized, he had two phones installed by his bedside so that he could carry on working. He was ordered to rest in bed for six months, but stayed for only six weeks. He reports that Shirley rarely visited him in this period, and was always cold and distant over the phone, and seemed swayed by literally everyone she talked to: if someone she knew sneered at Brighton, for example, Shirley then refused to ever sing there again. She was being showered with expensive gifts by rich admirers, while by contrast Sullivan was stopping large chunks of her income to make the payments on her mother's house. Tempers flared often, and Sullivan claims that Shirley once yelled at him, 'What good is a manager who's lying on his back all day?' At this point, Sullivan knew he had to do something drastic to stay in her favour.

Fortunately, an offer of work came in from Australia, and Sullivan decided to launch his star in yet another new territory. This meant going there in person himself, something which Sullivan's TB specialist was very unhappy about. As a compromise, Sullivan promised to make the journey in easy stages, with long rests between flights.

Meanwhile, Shirley had moved out of the Davies family home, as Pepe's mother no longer wanted her to stay there – her son was apparently distraught at having to watch Shirley constantly going off on dates with other men. Shirley next took a room at the Cumberland Hotel, near Marble Arch, which was conveniently close to her current booking, at the Bagatelle nightclub in Berkeley Square.

That November, Shirley was scheduled to undertake her first tour of Australia, and Sullivan flew out 10 days before her, to organize advance publicity at the other end. He spent his days appearing on local TV and radio stations and singing Shirley's praises, and also cultivating friendships with Australian journalists. On 10 November, the morning before Shirley was due to fly out to join him, Sullivan was woken up by a phone call at 3 a.m. from journalist Clyde Packer of the Sydney *Daily Telegraph*. Packer told him that bad news had just arrived from a news agency in England. All it said was: 'Shirley Bassey in shooting.' Sullivan immediately rushed to the *Daily Telegraph* office, but there was no more word. He tried phoning London, but without success. Eventually more news came through from the agency, although the details were sketchy: Shirley Bassey had been taken hostage in her hotel room by an armed gunman, and shots had been fired; no one knew for certain whether she was alive or dead.

six

s i x

THE HOSTAGE

The whole story, as Shirley later told it to Mike Sullivan, was this: the night before she was due to fly out to Australia, she'd gone to the cinema with Peter Quinton, a boy she'd been dating for a week or so. Afterwards, at around midnight he had accompanied her back to her hotel to help her pack; she was also expecting 'the boys' (her two dressmakers) to deliver a new gown for her that had been ordered for the tour. Then the phone rang, and a man with a phoney American accent told Shirley that he had some flowers to deliver to her; Shirley recognized the voice as belonging to Pepe Davies, and told him to give the flowers to his mother before putting the phone down on him.

She then went into the bathroom to remove her make-up, having told Quinton that if there was a knock on the door he should ask who it was before letting them in. A short while later Shirley heard her dressmakers arrive with her gown. Then, still in the bathroom, she heard another knock at the door, followed by some talking – and then she heard a gunshot.

She rushed back into the bedroom to discover that her dressmakers had already fled the scene, and Quinton was now struggling with Terence Davies – who was holding a gun. Quinton had blood streaming down his head. Shirley tried to separate the two men, and then felt the barrel of the gun jabbing into her stomach. Davies told her to get rid of Quinton, or else he'd pull the trigger. Shirley briefly explained the situation to Quinton and told him that he'd better leave – which he did, after first grabbing a towel to wrap around his head.

Davies quickly pushed a chest of drawers against the door of the room, adding some chairs and Shirley's big travel trunk to form a crude barricade. Then he picked up the telephone and made a call, forcing Shirley to 'tell his mother he was there and that he was going to kill me. She laughed and he grabbed the phone and spoke. I don't know what his mother said. Maybe she laughed at him too, but he fired into the telephone and it shattered all over the place.'

Then Peter Quinton came back, accompanied by several police officers. Shirley heard a dog barking outside her room, and detectives were banging on the door and shouting at Davies, telling him to let the girl go. The police had commandeered the room opposite Shirley's, so that they could see in through her window. Davies ignored them, and made Shirley play records; he wanted a drink, but all she had was a whisky liqueur, which he spat out after one sip. He sat on the bed, toying with the gun. Then he got up and pointed it directly at Shirley's head, demanding that she kiss him. When she refused, he threatened to pull the trigger. 'I don't care,' replied Shirley. Davies pulled the trigger, and Shirley fainted and fell down. The only reason that she wasn't dead was because while fiddling with the gun, Davies had moved the gun's chamber to one where there was no longer a bullet. This might have been done accidentally – but more probably, Davies had done it deliberately, wanting to give Shirley a nasty shock, since he afterwards swore that he'd never intended to harm her.

When Shirley came to, Davies again ordered her to kiss him, and this time she complied. Davies's father then arrived outside the room, and told his son to come out, that this girl just wasn't worth all the trouble. Davies fired the gun through the door and then sat down again on the bed, constantly jerking the gun up and down. Understandably, Shirley was terrified, and almost certainly believed she was going to die in this room.

Davies ordered Shirley to undress, and she began slowly removing her clothes. Davies had drawn the curtains, but Shirley thought people might still be able to see in from outside. She tried to stall him by changing the record and offering him another drink, but Davies wouldn't be distracted, insisting that she continue to undress; she stripped to her underwear and paused, but Davies ordered her to take everything off. He then pushed the naked Shirley onto the bed, and began to kiss her; she assumed that she was about to be raped.

At this point someone banged on the door, possibly concerned because everything had gone so quiet inside. Davies stood up and fired another shot through the door. 'By now I am hysterical,' Shirley told Sullivan. 'I'm pleading with him, practically on my hands and knees begging him to let me go.' It was then 2.45 in the morning, and she had been trapped alone with Davies for over two hours. To Shirley's surprise, at this point Davies suddenly announced that he was willing to let her go free, and he told the police outside the door that he was about to do so – but that if he saw any of them through the doorway he'd shoot to kill, and would shoot Shirley as well. The police agreed to leave.

Shirley asked Davies if she could get dressed again, and when he consented she hurriedly pulled on a skirt and sweater, not bothering to replace her underwear in her haste to cover herself up. Davies pulled all the piled-up furniture away from the door and pushed Shirley out into the corridor, where she collapsed. 'Someone picked me up and I remember seeing Peter with a towel around his head.' She was put to bed in another room, but couldn't sleep until a doctor gave her an injection.

After he had released Shirley, the police waited patiently outside the room where Davies was still holed up. After an hour, he pushed a handwritten suicide note under the door. It began, 'To whom it may concern, I love with all my heart Shirley Bassey, who is not to blame for this killing.' Believing that the reference to 'killing' meant that Davies was now about to shoot himself, the police quickly broke into the room. Later, when they took a statement from Shirley, detectives told her that Davies had been arrested, but had shot himself in the leg during the struggle.

The next morning Shirley was interviewed by the press, and was told that Davies was now claiming that she had consented to marry him while he was in hospital after his car crash. She told the *South Wales Echo* that Davies's claim was true, she had indeed agreed to marry the boy, 'but only because he was very ill. I only said it to help him get well.' She added that, 'Before the accident he was sweet and charming. I think it changed him.' During her ordeal, she said that Davies had told her, 'I love you but you don't love me,' and she had replied, 'I love you in my own funny way.' Another reporter told her that he had seen 'everything' through the window. 'And I was in the nude,' she later told Sullivan. 'Do you think that's what he meant by "everything"?'

*

As for Terence Davies, he had indeed shot himself in the leg, and had been taken to St Mary's Hospital near Paddington. According to Muriel Burgess, when cautioned at his bedside by Superintendent Marner, Davies told him that he loved Shirley, and hadn't intended to shoot her: 'I just went mad at the time and now I want to suffer.' When discharged from hospital he was taken into police custody; a few days later he made a brief appearance in court and was granted bail.

Davies's case came to trial at the Old Bailey several months later, while Shirley was still on tour in Australia. In the dock he repeated his claim that Shirley had agreed to marry him and said, 'I am devoted to her.' The defence claimed that Davies had sustained head injuries in his car accident, and had suffered brain damage as a result; he was thus not wholly responsible for his actions. The prosecuting counsel, Christmas Humphreys, insisted that Davies was just 'a stupid, silly, lovesick youth.' Summing up before passing sentence, Mr Justice Cassels said that Davies had been 'within a hair's breadth of almost having to stand trial for what would have been a charge of murder.' Davies was sentenced to three years in prison, and the severity of the sentence supposedly reflected the fact that the shots he had fired through the hotel door could easily have killed a policeman.

Davies's fate subsequent to his term in prison is unknown. Since his death has never been reported, we must presume that he is still alive.

*

In Australia, Michael Sullivan had only had to wait a few more hours before learning that Shirley was unhurt and free, but they were a bad few hours. Later that day he saw wired news photographs of her at London airport, boarding a plane for Australia; at Sydney airport the next day she was met by three TV crews and over 30 journalists eager to talk to her about her ordeal – but she was extremely tired and irritable, and in no mood to be interviewed. Her first words to Sullivan were, 'Fancy sending me tourist class on a 36-hour flight.' But the press were all around her, and there was no avoiding them; still, she wasn't inclined to play along, and her answers to their questions were downright abrasive. As she was attempting to leave the scene, Sullivan introduced Shirley to Bruce Gordon, the general manager of Sydney's Tivoli Theatre, where she would soon be appearing; he was tall and handsome, and quickly made an impression on Shirley. Sullivan retreated and let Gordon work his charms on Shirley, and soon she was even being amenable to the waiting radio reporters. According to Sullivan, this was the start of a relationship between Shirley and Gordon which soon 'developed into a warm love affair, and for a time there was even talk of marriage.'

Only the next day, after Shirley had rested, did she tell Sullivan the full story of her captivity. Within a few weeks she was more agreeable to the idea of talking to the press, and began giving interviews. The headline for one read: 'The trouble I've had with men.' In the article, Shirley related how, 'Everyone knows the trouble I had when my ex-boyfriend burst into my hotel room the night before I left to come here. I felt sorry for him. I liked him at first and went out with him for quite a while until I went to the States.' In the USA, she went on, she had met so many interesting men that by the time she got back to Britain she no longer found Davies appealing. She ruefully concluded, 'When a girl's reached the top she has to be careful of all kinds of things, but especially men.'

Sullivan and Shirley spent the next six months in Australia. He was still weak and ill, and had to spend half of each day in bed; even so, he recalls the period as being 'tolerably good', perhaps because 'Shirley and I did not have enough time together to clash in any serious way.' Sullivan had been joined in Australia by Lily, who had moved in with him; she was also appearing on the same bill as Shirley. As for Shirley, her spare time was all happily filled by her relationship with Bruce Gordon – although according to Sullivan, 'when Bruce was not around she was having an affair with a good-looking layabout called Peter.' It sounds as if Sullivan is implying that Shirley began her affair with the Australian actor Peter Finch during this tour, but that seems rather unlikely, and contradicts other reports.

Despite the fact that she was enjoying herself, at Christmas time Shirley became extremely homesick. She told Sullivan, 'This is the first time I've not been at home with the family for Christmas. I've always had a pillowcase full of presents at the bottom of my bed.' That night Sullivan and Lily scoured Sydney in search of a Santa Claus costume; when they finally found one, they had to get the shop owner out of bed in order to rent it. A few hours later Shirley was terrified when she woke up just before dawn to discover a hooded man in her room – and relieved to find that it was only Lily dressed up as Santa Claus, delivering a pillowcase stuffed with presents that she and Sullivan had bought for the homesick girl.

*

In January 1958, while in Sydney, Shirley turned 21, and was now legally an adult. To mark the occasion, Sullivan finally gave in to one of her more repeated requests; he told her that he'd ordered a white Jaguar sports car for her. It would be delivered as soon as they returned to England.

It must have seemed to Shirley as if she was on top of the world now, with her night of danger well behind her: she had a good relationship, a new car, a successful career and the weather was beautiful – and then the sky caved in on her. One day Shirley was contacted by the Sydney correspondent of the British newspaper the *Daily Sketch*, and asked if she could be in her hotel room at a certain time to receive a phone call from the *Sketch* office in London. She was apparently told that this was to do with a story about how much she was enjoying her stay in Australia. Sullivan was mystified when he heard about this, as it seemed like something the Sydney correspondent could easily have handled himself. Still, he thought no more of it, and when the phone call didn't come at the agreed time that afternoon, he decided to go to the cinema. Halfway through the main film, Sullivan's name was flashed up on the screen, with a message telling him to go to the Tivoli Theatre immediately. There he found Shirley 'in hysterics', and learned that she had broken down in tears on stage in mid-song, and had been unable to resume her performance.

He took her back to her hotel, calmed her down and was finally told what had happened. The *Sketch* had eventually called, shortly after Sullivan had left for the cinema, and for Shirley their reason for telephoning could not possibly have been worse. As Sullivan had predicted long before, Shirley's fame had inevitably attracted the attentions of the seedier end of Fleet Street, and it hadn't taken the *Sketch* long to find out about Sharon's existence. They had even acquired a copy of her birth certificate, and their telephone call had been to inform Shirley that they were planning to publish these facts in a story about her on Monday – two days from now. Did she have any comment?

Shirley's secret was finally about to come out, and nothing could stop it. Sullivan reasoned that their best hope of surviving the scandal was to beat the *Daily Sketch* to the post, by publicly revealing the truth about Sharon themselves. He rang a journalist in London whom he knew to be friendly, Arthur Helliwell of the *People*. Even though the paper was one of England's two main Sunday 'scandal sheets' at the time, it also had one great advantage; being a Sunday paper, it would come out one day before the *Daily Sketch*, and hopefully prevent at least some of the damage the *Sketch* piece would otherwise cause. Sullivan briefed Helliwell on the situation, offering him an exclusive interview with Shirley if he agreed to treat her sympathetically. Helliwell did so, and conducted a 45-minute phone interview with Shirley in which she told him all about the circumstances of Sharon's birth, how she had refused to give her baby up for adoption and struggled to raise her herself, how her daughter was now being raised by her sister and how much she missed her little girl. Sullivan's ploy worked, and Helliwell's interview with Shirley appeared in print the next day – as a result of which the *Daily Sketch* piece, which would almost certainly have been far less kind, never appeared at all.

Sullivan was still concerned as to what public reaction would be like in Australia, which was a far more conservative country than Britain in those days – a fact that resulted in numerous young Australians (Barry Humphries, Clive James and Germaine Greer among them) permanently moving to London during the 1950s and 1960s. Sullivan used the same tactics as before, arranging for Shirley to tell her version of events to a sympathetic Australian magazine, which ran the interview under a headline that read, 'Give her a break.' Fortunately, the Australian audiences seemed to feel the same way, and Shirley was given an enthusiastic welcome the next time she took to the stage. Sullivan thought that the whole issue must have completely faded away a month later, when he and Shirley were invited to a garden party that was being held in Sydney for the Queen Mother; they didn't manage to actually meet her at the event, but in itself their invitation seemed a sign that Shirley wasn't a complete social outcast after all. Even so, between the Terence Davies situation and the revelations about Sharon, Sullivan feared that Shirley might still face a frosty reception when she got back to London.

Just before their planned return to England, Shirley was taken ill in Melbourne with a grumbling appendix. She was advised to take things easy, and not to go swimming. This was a real blow, since Sullivan had arranged for them to fly home via Hawaii and

San Francisco. In California, Sullivan planned to have some meetings with Hollywood agents about future work for Shirley, but the Hawaii stopover was intended to be simply a beach holiday. They stayed at the Reef Hotel in Honolulu, and to his credit Sullivan realized that it would be rather unfair if he and Lily splashed around in the surf while Shirley just watched them from the beach, so he promised her that neither he nor Lily would swim if she didn't. This agreement lasted for several days – until Sullivan caught Shirley sneaking a quiet solo swim in the hotel swimming pool.

That night Shirley knocked on the door of Sullivan's room and told him she wasn't feeling at all well. 'I found her twisted with pain, and thinking it might be simply stomach cramps from the swimming I gave her three sleeping pills. An hour later she called again and I went to her room. She was sweating, crying and obviously in great pain. I got the hotel reception desk to call a doctor and waited with Shirley,' Sullivan wrote later. The doctor gave Shirley some medicine to get her through the night, and saw her again the next morning, when he told her that it was essential she consult a specialist as soon as she got back home.

When they left Hawaii, Shirley and Sullivan had 'a flaming row over money, because she had overspent and did not have enough money to cover her hotel bill.' Sullivan refused to pay, to teach her a lesson, and Shirley stormed off; but before he went up to his room to pack Sullivan put an envelope containing $100 in Shirley's key slot at the reception desk. When he checked out of the hotel he discovered the envelope was still there, but that Shirley had already checked out and gone to the airport. Sullivan assumed that Shirley must have had enough money after all, and had paid her bill herself. He retrieved the envelope and left for the airport with Lily.

On the flight to California, Sullivan and Shirley did not talk at all. When they landed at San Francisco airport Sullivan was stopped by an airline official and informed that they had received a cable from the Reef Hotel to the effect that Shirley had left there without paying her bill. Bizarrely, instead of just paying the bill himself, or giving Shirley the envelope containing the money as he had originally intended, Sullivan now threw her to the wolves. He pointed Shirley out to the airline official and walked calmly off to retrieve his luggage. A few minutes later the official sought him out again and told him that Shirley had said that he would pay her bill. Not only did Sullivan refuse to do so, he refused to even speak to her.

Sullivan didn't see Shirley again until several weeks later, when he returned from Hollywood. But he did receive a note from her the next day at his hotel, which read: 'I hope you're feeling happy with what you've done. May God forgive you, because I never will.' Given subsequent events, perhaps she never did. That morning Sullivan also learned that Shirley had arranged to pay the outstanding hotel bill through her bank in London, had somehow scraped up enough cash to pay for one night in the San Francisco hotel, and had now flown back to England. Though Sullivan didn't know it at the time, Shirley had also had a recurrence of her appendix trouble while in San Francisco; however, he was still concerned enough about the state of her health to arrange for his associate, Leonard Beresford Clark, to meet Shirley's plane at London airport, and to take care of her. When she arrived, Shirley was so ill that Clark took her back to his home in Reigate, where she remained under medical supervision for a month, until her abdominal pains had subsided.

After this, relations between Shirley and Sullivan were understandably strained for some months to come. She got her Jaguar, as he had promised, but given the circumstances he wisely decided not to make a press event out of the car's arrival. But whatever their feelings about each other now, work went on. Sullivan booked Shirley into another Leslie Grade variety tour, which was due to open at the Chiswick Empire. 'As I discussed terms with Leslie I promised him that I would get some sort of a story in the newspapers reminding a forgetful nation that Shirley Bassey still existed,' Sullivan later reported. The scheme that he concocted was definitely one of his dafter ideas, and one could have easily guessed that it would backfire. Sullivan wanted Shirley to disappear completely from sight. He would then report her to the police as a missing person, which would result in headline coverage in the national newspapers, who would continue to cover the search for her. When she miraculously turned up safe and sound again, there would be yet more headlines.

Shirley thought the idea was ridiculous. For one thing, she was far too well known now to pass unrecognized anywhere in Britain; and if she left the country, there would be a record of her departure somewhere. Sullivan told her that she wasn't 'the only coloured girl in Britain', and joked that no one would recognize her if she dressed smartly. What about the new songs she was working on, Shirley wanted to know. How was she supposed to have them ready for the tour if she couldn't rehearse them properly? Sullivan promised her that he'd supply her with a tape of the piano accompaniments; she could then rehearse wherever she was. This didn't seem to take into account the fact that some stranger might overhear Shirley Bassey singing and blow the whole thing. Sullivan would not be deterred. He and Shirley arranged to meet a few days later in the bar of the Mapleton Hotel, where he was still living.

At the meeting in the Mapleton were the four people who were to be in on the secret: Sullivan and Shirley, Shirley's secretary David Gilmour, and Joan Pound, a trusted friend of Sullivan's who was to accompany Shirley to her destination. Sullivan had decided that this would be Bath, since it was a fairly sleepy town with no obvious connection to himself or Shirley; it was also close enough to London for her to make a speedy return when the time came. For all the stupidity of his plan, Sullivan might just have got away with it . . . but when he asked the Mapleton's receptionist for a train timetable, the receptionist asked if there was anything he could look up for him, Sullivan foolishly replied that he wanted to know the train times to Bath. Finding Shirley would thus hardly be hard work for any journalist worth their salt.

Shirley was due to open at the Chiswick Empire on a Monday night. On the Thursday morning of the previous week, she and Joan, conservatively dressed, boarded a train for Bath. When they arrived, they checked into a suitably quiet hotel. Sullivan let two days pass, and then went to London's West End Central police station on Saturday morning and reported Shirley missing. He claimed that she had failed to keep a rehearsal appointment two days previously, and had not been seen at her hotel since. Neither he, nor anyone else connected with Shirley, had heard a word from her. He thought perhaps she had gone to Cardiff to visit her mother, but she usually told him of such visits . . . and it would be very unlike Shirley to take time off so close to opening in a new show. The police sergeant noted down Eliza's address and asked whether Sullivan had quarrelled with his client recently. He admitted that they had, but explained that this was nothing unusual; Shirley would still have turned up to rehearsals, he insisted. The sergeant told Sullivan to leave the matter with them, and to call back in a few hours.

When Sullivan telephoned the police that afternoon, they told him they had checked with Cardiff. Shirley was not at her mother's house, nor was she expected there. Sullivan now said that he was extremely concerned, and reminded the officer that Shirley had already been abducted once. 'He vaguely remembered this, and it helped to convince him that I was genuinely worried,' Sullivan later recalled. The police said they would put Shirley on the missing person's list, and asked Sullivan to supply a photograph. Sullivan gladly agreed to do so, and asked whether they should supply a copy to the press, since Shirley was such a public figure. The police agreed to contact the newspapers, 'which was just what I was praying for. I wanted this stunt to be as official as possible.'

For the next two days Sullivan's office was besieged by the press, and the telephone never stopped ringing. On Saturday evening Shirley's disappearance made the TV news, and the Sunday papers were full of it the next day. It was beginning to look as if Sullivan's plan had worked; he'd got all the news coverage he'd hoped for, and had undoubtedly made the British public aware that Shirley Bassey was back from Australia.

Of course, it couldn't last. Ironically, it was a reporter from the *Daily Sketch*, Jack Lewis, who tracked Shirley to Bath, by the simple expedient of talking to the receptionist at the Mapleton. When confronted by Lewis, Sullivan tried bluffing, 'but the following day the paper carried a story which indicated I had admitted everything. I had not, but after Australia I had to grant them some licence, and we were pegging level,' Sullivan conceded. For the *Daily Sketch*, it was doubtless a sweet revenge.

Despite the *Sketch* story, Sullivan continued to bluff his way through Monday, right up until the moment that Shirley arrived at the Chiswick Empire, wondering why everyone was surprised to see her: 'Me missing? I just went away for a rest.' Her concert that night would be a triumph, and the next day's papers would put the story to rest in style. At least, that was the plan. Then Shirley had an egg thrown at her on stage; it missed her by yards, and she was blissfully unaware of it, believing that someone had thrown her a flower. The culprit was never caught, and the next day the newspaper stories all reported that Shirley had been pelted with eggs on stage.

'Anyone who says "no publicity is bad" is an idiot,' Sullivan later wrote.

That one egg was a disaster. It ruined the effect I had carefully built up over Shirley's disappearance and it kept people away from the theatre. On Monday the takings at Chiswick were £400. Through the week they dropped to £100, £70 and, finally, to £60. People put on their best clothes for the theatre and they don't want to risk getting in the way of an egg, even if it is meant for somebody else.

After the *Daily Sketch* story appeared, the police summoned Sullivan back to West End Central, where he was given a severe talking-to; they couldn't exactly prove that he had manipulated them for his own ends, but they had their suspicions, and warned him of the dire consequences if they should obtain such proof, or if he should ever pull a stunt like this in the future. Sullivan continued to deny everything, but thanked the police for the warning and left as soon as he could, 'trying not to look too guilty.'

The following week the variety tour took Shirley to Birmingham, where the pains in her side returned once again. She was taken to hospital at two in the morning, and a doctor phoned Sullivan in London to tell him the news. Despite his awareness of all of Shirley's previous problems with her appendix, this time Sullivan doubted that there was anything actually wrong with her; she was probably just malingering, he thought, wanting some time off after the Chiswick egg and her subsequent roasting in the press. But the doctor told him that Shirley was very definitely extremely ill, and he was awaiting the arrival of a specialist consultant. Sullivan was told to call back in an hour for an update. 'I sweated out the hour and when I called the hospital I was told she had peritonitis and an immediate operation was vital. Without it she could die, and even with it there was no guarantee.'

The operation went ahead to remove Shirley's ruptured appendix, and she remained on the danger list for a short time afterwards. She was unable to work for at least six weeks, a period during which she recuperated once again at Leonard Beresford Clark's house in Reigate. Sullivan was forced to cancel the rest of the Grade tour, and all the other engagements for Shirley that he'd lined up to follow it. This was extremely fortunate for all concerned, because advance ticket sales for all the dates had slumped to practically zero.

THE LONG GOODBYE

Between her abduction, the press revelations of Sharon's existence and her several bouts of appendix-related illness, Shirley Bassey had suffered through what was probably the worst six months of her life to date. Worse still, after she recovered from her operation the bad luck seemed to continue; now Sullivan found it impossible to get her any work, since no one wanted to book her. He got round the problem by promoting Shirley's next British tour himself, but it was only a temporary solution. 'Shirley sang as well as ever on that tour,' he later wrote, 'but the telephone was silent. I had to find a way to start it ringing again.'

The method Sullivan used to kick-start Shirley's stalled career was little short of blackmail. That summer's biggest British show-business event was expected to be *The Night of a Hundred Stars*, a televised charity fundraiser from the London Palladium in late July which would feature the top stars of the day and be hosted by Sir Laurence Olivier. Sullivan rang the organizers of the event and expressed surprise that Shirley Bassey had not been invited to participate in the show. Surely this couldn't be a question of colour prejudice? 'I was gambling on my infamous reputation of rushing to the newspapers with any story that I thought would raise some dust, and I knew that no reputable body would like to be tainted with the cry of "colour bar",' Sullivan later recounted. Within minutes of his call, Shirley's name had been added to the bill.

As always when the chips were down, on the night Shirley gave of her utmost. She made a dramatic entrance, walking down a huge staircase and wearing one of her most revealing new gowns while singing 'The Birth of the Blues', accompanied by 'the man with the golden trumpet', Eddie Calvert. The performance was all that Sullivan could have hoped for, and it re-established Shirley Bassey in the public's mind as being one of the most sensational entertainers in the country. The next day, Sullivan later reported with triumph, 'my silent telephone got its voice back,' and Shirley soon had a string of new bookings lined up.

*

In 1957, Shirley's debut album *Born To Sing The Blues* had been released, but she had been unhappy with the producer's choice of material; from now on, she wanted to be able to choose at least some of her songs herself. In mid-1958 Shirley recorded two songs that would radically affect her career for the better; the first of these was a smoochy ballad she had discovered herself, 'As I Love You', written in 1955 by Ray Evans and Jay Livingston (who had also penned numerous other 1950s hits, including 'Buttons and Bows', 'Mona Lisa' and 'Que Sera, Sera'), which despite being recorded by several American artists (including a version by Joe Williams with the Count Basie Orchestra), had never been a hit. Shirley's version is extremely impressive, partly because in her performance she gave of her all, and partly because producer Johnny Franz gave the song an innovative arrangement reminiscent of the early work of Burt Bacharach – but Shirley had to work hard to persuade Franz to let her record the song at all. What he required at that point was something to serve as the B-side to another ballad, 'Hands Across the Sea', and the music industry's received wisdom at the time had it that you couldn't put two ballads back to back. It took two weeks for Shirley to talk Franz around, but afterwards they both knew they'd created something special.

At the end of the year Shirley sang the song during her appearance on TV's *Saturday Night at The London Palladium*, and in February 1959, 'As I Love You' went to number one in the charts. Her next single, recorded at around the same time, followed almost immediately. 'Kiss Me Honey, Honey Kiss Me' was a saucily flirtatious novelty number, lightweight but fun, which featured backing vocals by Shirley's musical director at the time, Kenny Clayton. Still, when compared to her performance on 'As I Love You', it not only sounds like inconsequential fluff, but also as if Shirley's heart isn't really in it. Although she still performs the song in her live act to this day, it's now transformed into a piece of knowing camp, as Shirley glides across the stage in a seductive shimmy.

'Kiss Me' quickly followed 'As I Love You' up the charts, both songs appearing in the top three at the same time. It was the kind of success most singers can only dream of, and almost unheard of in those pre-Beatle days – and Shirley was still only 22 years old. Both songs were also included on her next album, *The Bewitching Miss Bassey*, as were 'Burn My Candle' and 'The Banana Boat

Song' (the balance of the album being mainly a collection of standards).

To fuel the chart race between 'Kiss Me' and 'As I Love You', Michael Sullivan insisted that both songs be given equal opportunity, and that Shirley should alternate between them when making promotional TV and radio appearances. On one TV show (Joe Loss's *Top Twenty Show*, according to Muriel Burgess), Shirley was scheduled to plug 'Kiss Me', but during rehearsals announced that she was heartily sick of the song, and would be performing 'As I Love You' instead. The show's producer consulted with Sullivan, who was ill in bed, and annoyed that Shirley was bucking their agreement. Sullivan promptly had sent over to the TV studio the sheet music for only one song, 'Kiss Me Honey, Honey Kiss Me', thus making a performance of 'As I Love You' impossible. It was Sullivan's way of reminding Shirley who was boss, but although she grudgingly went ahead and sang 'Kiss Me' on the show, she was understandably furious with him.

*

In late 1958, while on a trip to Cardiff to see her mother and Sharon, Shirley had paid a visit to a nightclub in the town owned by a friend of hers, Annis Abraham. Here she met for the first time Abraham's two business partners, Clive Sharp and Maurice King, who also owned The Showbiz Club, a new venue in London which Shirley visited soon afterwards – and not long after that, she and Sharp began dating. She even took him to a Christmas party at Michael Sullivan's house, but her manager paid him no more attention than he did any of Shirley's other boyfriends after Davies.

Meanwhile, Sullivan had seen a revue show in Blackpool called *The Folies-Bergère* that he thought would make a perfect stage vehicle for Shirley. He bought the rights to the show, renamed it *Blue Magic*, and began making arrangements for it to open in London.

By early 1959 *Blue Magic* was booked to open in the spring at the Prince of Wales Theatre, practically opposite the Café de Paris. It was billed as 'a gay new glamour revue'; Shirley would be the star of the show, and among the other acts on the bill would be the conjuring comedian Tommy Cooper. To make sure Shirley was well versed in the new songs she would be premiering in *Blue Magic*, just before the show was due to open Sullivan booked her into a week's run in a variety show in Colchester. During that week he paid her several visits, and each time discovered two young men in her dressing room – 'two young "faces" who ran a drinking club in Soho', in Sullivan's words. They were Clive Sharp and Maurice King, and despite Sullivan's request for a quiet word alone, Shirley insisted that, 'It's perfectly all right. Anything you wish to say can be said in front of these gentlemen.'

The following week, after Shirley had failed to show up at the theatre for the first two *Blue Magic* rehearsals, Sullivan confronted her at her new flat in Dolphin Square, overlooking the Thames between Pimlico and Chelsea. Shirley told Sullivan straight out that she thought he had been taking too much money from her, and that normally a manager was only entitled to 20 per cent of his client's earnings. Sullivan replied that he'd be happy to take only 20 per cent as long as he no longer had to 'pay out for agents' commissions, fares, new music, costumes, flowers, hire of jewellery, entertainment and all the other things I have been finding money for.' They eventually agreed to tear up their old contracts and sign new ones. Sullivan instructed the solicitor who was acting for both of them to draw up a contract between Shirley and James Bauries, the producer of *Blue Magic*, and to also draw up a new contract between himself and Shirley, under the terms of which he would receive 20 per cent of her earnings.

At this point, as soon as she had signed the *Blue Magic* contract Shirley informed Sullivan that he was 'finished' – she no longer wanted him as her manager. He warned her that he would sue her, and she responded that her original contract 'had been illegal all along', presumably because she had signed it while still a minor. Within days, Shirley had appointed Clive Sharp and Maurice King as her new managers, and Jock Jacobson as her new agent. Michael Sullivan had to pay for his own ticket for the opening night of *Blue Magic*, and Clive Sharp had him banned from entering the theatre's backstage area. It seemed that the Sullivan/Bassey dispute would now be decided in court.

Within months of scoring her chart successes with 'As I Love You' and 'Kiss Me Honey, Honey Kiss Me', Shirley left Philips Records and signed a new recording deal with EMI in Britain and Columbia in the USA. This was definitely a step upward, since both companies were prestigious record labels; at this point EMI were the most successful record company in Britain, a position they'd soon consolidate for decades to come by signing both Cliff Richard and (through their subsidiary label Parlophone) the Beatles. Muriel Burgess credits Kenneth Hume as being the instigator of Shirley's label change, but since Hume didn't enter the picture for nearly two more years, this is clearly impossible.

Above: A dream came true for sixteen-year-old Shirley when she was singing in a Cardiff working men's club and spotted by local booking agent Georgie Wood. He recommended that she be auditioned for a part in the 'Memories of Jolson' stage show, which eventually opened at the Grand Theatre in Luton in 1953.

Left: By 1956, Shirley was appearing on TV and radio shows, singing nightly in cabaret and rubbing shoulders with household names such as Tommy Trinder.

Left: Dress designer Douglas Darnell puts the finishing touches to one of Shirley's stage outfits in 1960. The sheath dress was covered in 156,000 diamante stones and weighed 28 lbs (13 kg).

Left: Radio comedy star Al Read helps Shirley cut the cake to celebrate her nineteenth birthday at the Adelphi Theatre in London, where she was appearing with Read in 'Such is Life'.

Right: Shirley walks off with a gold disc awarded, according to the label, for achieving 'Two million dollars in album sales Goldfinger Original Motion Picture 1965 Soundtrack'.

Left: Shirley married
Kenneth Hume in 1961
declaring that she was
madly in love with him
despite the fact that he
was a homosexual. She
even forgave him when
she caught him in bed
with their chauffeur
shortly after their
marriage. The couple
divorced in 1965,
although he continued
to work as her manager.

Left: Shirley at London
Airport in 1966 with
daughters Sharon and
Samantha. She resolutely
refused to name the
fathers of her girls.

Right: Shirley wore a number of specially-designed stage dresses that were either revealing, see-through or both. When she asked designer Douglas Darnell what she should wear under one creation he replied, 'As little as possible.' The cutaway number seen here was banned from American TV in 1967.

Left: Shirley with former hotel manager Sergio Novak, who became her husband in 1968 and her manager shortly afterwards. Shirley's daughters were to adopt the Novak surname.

Above: Shirley with Prince Charles on his thirty-first birthday following a gala charity performance at Wembley Conference Centre in 1979. Her top was see-through and, predictably, there was only Shirley underneath.

Above: Shirley pictured with Mark, the grandson of her sister, Ella, in 1982. Shirley and Sergio Novak had adopted Mark as their own son many years before.

Left: Shirley at the funeral of her daughter, Samantha, who died as the result of a tragic accident in 1985, having fallen into the River Avon at Bristol after having been out drinking with friends.

Right: Prior to the announcement of the New Year's Honours List at the end of 1999, Shirley had to keep the news about her damehood a secret for seven weeks and was 'afraid to go out in case I told someone.'

Above: Fifty of Dame Shirley's most glamorous stage outfits, representing her amazing fifty years in showbusiness, were auctioned for charity by Christie's in London in 2003.

Left: Dame Shirley captivated the Glastonbury Festival in June 2007, paying tribute to the thousands floundering in the Glastonbury mud by accessorizing her stage outfit with customized wellies.

Although the deal could have been struck by Clive Sharp and Maurice King, it seems far more likely that it was – at the very least – set in motion by Michael Sullivan.

As her first release on EMI, Shirley contributed to a rather strange LP on their subsidiary label HMV, which – despite the fact that this version was never staged in the theatre – was a studio recording of the score to the Jerome Kern musical *Showboat* (the only other 'name' in the cast besides Shirley being the comedy actress Dora Bryan). Unsurprisingly, Shirley took the role of Julie (portrayed in the two film versions of the musical by Helen Morgan and Ava Gardner respectively), delivering creditable versions of 'Can't Help Lovin' Dat Man' and 'Bill.' Shirley alone is portrayed on the record's sleeve, looking suitably sultry.

Her first 'proper' LP for the label was *The Fabulous Shirley Bassey*, which began her long-running relationships with both producer Norman Newell and musical director Geoff Love. The material consisted mainly of standards, as did her first few single releases. In the main they were competently handled, but not that remarkable.

The next year, 1960, brought her better luck. A cover of 'With These Hands' charted on three separate occasions, peaking at number 38. Shirley's biggest hit single to date followed almost immediately with 'As Long As He Needs Me', the love song from Lionel Bart's musical *Oliver* (backed with an extremely good version of Cole Porter's 'So In Love'). The record reached number two (it was kept from the top slot by Elvis Presley's 'Now Or Never', which was impossible competition to beat), and remained in the charts for 30 weeks. A few years later Shirley harboured

121

hopes of taking her association with the song a step further by actually playing the role of Nancy in the big screen version of *Oliver*,
but these were to be dashed; perhaps the producers felt that cinema
audiences in those days simply wouldn't accept a 'coloured' Nancy
(though the role has been played by at least one black actress in
recent years). Curiously, when the casting for the film role finally
did take place, the producers instead chose the comparatively
unknown Shari Wallis, who was at one time a client of Michael
Sullivan. Small world.

That spring, Shirley also appeared at London's Pigalle club. In
addition to her performance, patrons could also enjoy a three-course
dinner, dancing and a floorshow for the bargain price of 47 shillings
and sixpence (equivalent to about £60 today). In May, Shirley
appeared as the special guest of Anthony Newley on a TV show to
celebrate his Variety Club award for 'Most Promising Newcomer of
1959'. Newley and Shirley duetted – and ad-libbed – on a version of
'If You Were The Only Girl In The World', and the two got along
famously; Shirley also became lifelong friends with Newley's wife
Joan Collins, while her friend Peter Charlesworth became Newley's
confidant and 'unofficial manager' from then on. It's even possible
that it was at Shirley's suggestion that Newley was approached by
John Barry to write the lyrics for 'Goldfinger' a few years later.

Otherwise, life continued much as it had when she was with
Michael Sullivan, and as it would for decades to come. As she has
continued to do, every year Shirley usually toured in Australia, the
USA and Europe; a few decades later she would eventually conquer
Japan as well. She was in the USA during the run-up to the 1960
presidential election, and watched the televised debates between

John F. Kennedy and Richard Nixon with great interest, later describing herself as a 'great admirer' of Kennedy: 'He came across so strongly on television that he glowed, and that personality!' She could scarcely have dreamt at the time that one day she would meet both men in the flesh (she performed in front of Kennedy, and was also photographed with Nixon after he eventually became President himself). Before leaving the country, Shirley made her first national American TV appearance, on the *Ed Sullivan Show*.

*

As for Michael Sullivan, ever since *Blue Magic* had opened he had 'walked around with a Bassey-shaped hole in my heart – and my pocket.' He was suing Shirley for £8,000, tax-free – nearly £300,000 in today's terms. But – because his contract with Shirley had been an exclusive one – Sullivan was unable to act as a manager for any other artist until the case was finally heard in court. He had 'dabbled in show business' when opportunities arose, and had also managed a strip club in St James's – presumably an up-market strip club, given the location, but it was still somewhat of a comedown, as career moves go.

A date for the court case between Sullivan and Shirley was finally set, for 8 January 1961. Three weeks before then, in the early hours of 14 December 1960, Sullivan was woken up by a phone call from Shirley, requesting that they meet. He assumed that she was hoping to talk him out of going through with the court case, which he felt he had a good chance of winning, but – probably out of curiosity – he still agreed to an evening meeting at Shirley's house a few days later. When consulted, Sullivan's solicitor had no objection to this meeting going ahead, as long as it commenced with the standard legal declaration 'without prejudice.'

When Sullivan arrived at Shirley's new home, a terraced house in Stanhope Place, just opposite Hyde Park, he was amused to note that her doorbell chimed out a 'bing-bong' version of 'As I Love You'. Outside, Shirley's white Jaguar had evidently been replaced by the parked red Chevrolet convertible. Shirley's German house-keeper Gerda showed Sullivan through the deeply carpeted hall and up the stairs to where Shirley was waiting. 'Shirley stood at the door of the first-floor sitting room wearing an ankle-length brown velvet robe and a haughty, man-eating expression which she subconsciously puts on to face any new or uncomfortable experi-ence,' Sullivan later recalled. 'The haughtiness melted as I reached the doorway. Her arms opened and she hugged me. Feeling very foolish, I said: "Without prejudice." She laughed. "Oh yes, without prejudice".' They made awkward chit-chat for 10 minutes or so, and then Sullivan asked Shirley outright what she wanted.

Sullivan reports that Shirley told him, 'You always treated me like a child. Like a freak. You arranged things without telling me and I only used to find out about them when somebody else told me or I read about them somewhere. I know now that you were trying to save me from disappointment if things didn't materialize, but at the time I used to think you were doing things behind my back. People said to me, "He's deceiving you", and I believed them. They said, "You're the star. He only works for you".' She went on to tell Sullivan how much she had enjoyed her first year away from him – she had approved her own bookings, had made all her own decisions about clothes and music, and had generally relished her freedom. But at some point Shirley's relationship with Clive Sharp and Maurice King had soured. In the end their management style had evidently not been 'hands on' enough, and the fact that they had other business interests besides her meant that Shirley had felt neglected. She now once again wanted a manager to be someone who would give her their exclusive attention, and she wanted that person to be Michael Sullivan.

He could scarcely believe it. To cheer him up, his friends had been telling him for months that Shirley would change her tune one day, and would want him back again. Now that it had actually happened, Sullivan

> . . . tried to think calmly about her offer. Shirley Bassey, the singer, was my creation and I badly wanted her back, to guide her career and carry her forward to the place I had always had in mind for her, among the top stars in the world. On the other hand, she had been a damned nuisance. Looking after her had wrecked my health once and could easily do so again. I told her some of this and she swore she had changed, that she was more placid, more sensible, more mature. She seemed to be telling the truth.

Sullivan did not agree immediately. Instead, it took a week's worth of discussions and negotiations – including one meeting with Shirley and Jock Jacobson that Sullivan walked out of – before they finally agreed terms. Sullivan dropped his claim against Shirley for monies due from £8,000 tax-free to £6,000; of this, one third would be deducted from commissions yet to be earned, but Shirley would pay the tax due on it. Otherwise, their contract would be along exactly the same lines they had agreed nearly two years previously, with Sullivan receiving 20 per cent of Shirley's earnings. 'We signed the deal at her solicitor's office,' Sullivan reported. 'She turned up 10 minutes late for the meeting, signed the contract without reading a line of it, kissed me and breezed out.'

Their reunion would not last for long. Three weeks after signing the contract, Sullivan and Shirley departed for a two-month tour of Australia. Things went absolutely fine, until one night when Sullivan 'saw red.' Shirley was performing in a club, and was visibly 'seething' on stage because of the noisy chatter that was emanating from one table in the audience; as a result of this, she cut her set short by one song, leaving the stage five minutes earlier than on previous nights. Sullivan felt the audience had been cheated, even if they weren't aware of the fact, and burst into Shirley's dressing room to give her a dressing-down. He found her in fighting mood, insisting, 'If I had walked off in the middle of a number you would have something to complain about. For all they know I finished my act. You have no argument. The only time I can do what I want is when I am on that stage. Then I'm the boss.' She ordered him to leave her dressing room, and kicked him in the rear as he did so. The argument continued afterwards in the bar, and became worse when Shirley started drinking. Sullivan gave up and retired to bed, but was repeatedly woken up during the night by taunting phone calls from a drunken Shirley. The next day they made up again, and the rest of their Australian stay ran more smoothly.

*

On their way back to Britain in March 1961, Sullivan and Shirley stopped off for a few days' rest and relaxation in New York. Within hours of their arrival in the hotel there, Shirley happily announced that she'd bumped into someone in the lobby whom she knew from London – but as Michael Sullivan would later describe it, this was 'a meeting that was to develop into one of the most tragic periods of Shirley's life.' The man in question was Kenneth Hume, a director of TV commercials, whom Shirley had first met while filming one of her earliest TV appearances. Hume was 11 years older than Shirley (at the very least), but since she was often attracted to father figures this was not an obstacle to her seeing him as a romantic prospect; Hume was also several inches shorter than her, and several people who knew him have described his manner as comparable to that of a 'Cockney barrow boy.' None of this deterred Shirley's interest in Hume, but one thing should have done: he was also quite obviously gay, and seemingly made no secret of the fact (although homosexuality was still a criminal offence in Britain in those days, it was more or less openly accepted within the world of show business). Michael Sullivan, who had also known Hume in London, later delivered his fairly damning verdict of the man's character: 'He was homosexual, full of charm, two-faced and thoroughly detestable.'

He was also about to oust Michael Sullivan from Shirley's orbit for good.

eight

THE HUSBAND

Michael Sullivan paid very little attention to the almost constant presence of Kenneth Hume by Shirley's side in New York, as at the time he was busily negotiating – through transatlantic phone calls – a six-week season for Shirley at Blackpool Opera House. He also saw little harm in Shirley spending her time with a gay man, since 'Shirley always liked her men masculine' and he therefore thought that Hume could pose no serious threat to him. 'I should have taken more notice,' he later wrote. 'By our fourth day in the hotel Hume was actively courting Shirley and she was lapping up all the fawning attention he was paying to her.'

Even so, back in London, Sullivan still found it impossible to take this new relationship seriously – until some weeks later, when he received a phone call late one evening from John Mills, the owner of Les Ambassadeurs nightclub on Park Lane. Mills informed Sullivan that Shirley Bassey was in his club and had just publicly announced her engagement to Kenneth Hume. Sullivan asked Mills to send a bottle of champagne to their table with his congratulations.

The following day Hume and Shirley turned up together in a rented Rolls-Royce for her concert in Leicester. Sullivan was convinced that Hume was simply a gold-digger after Shirley's money, and did his best to discourage Shirley from going through with this prospective marriage with the brutally blunt observation: 'Look, it can't work. He's queer.' He suggested that if it was sex she wanted, she should go and have an affair with someone else, and forget Hume completely, but his advice went unheeded. According to Muriel Burgess, Shirley's former lover Bernard Hall had been bisexual, so perhaps she naively assumed that Hume's sexuality wouldn't be a major obstacle to their marriage succeeding; however, it would seem that Hume's tastes were predominantly homosexual, which was apparently not the case with Hall. 'Shirley was really in love with Hume, she was convinced she could change him and wanted to marry,' Sullivan later summed up. 'I dared not argue any more with her. All I could do was pray that she would come to her senses. She did not, and they married.'

The wedding did not take place until June. The month before, Shirley and Kenneth attended the 1961 Cannes Film Festival and stayed at the Carlton, the most expensive hotel in town. According to numerous reports, Hume was a phenomenally successful gambler, with a talent for roulette which he demonstrated at the local casinos – legend has it that he even successfully played three roulette tables simultaneously.

Kenneth Hume and Shirley Bassey married shortly after 9.30 on the morning of 8 June 1961, at Paddington registrar's office. The bride arrived in Hume's coffee-coloured Bentley, and wore a pink costume with matching toque hat and veil. The groom arrived on foot two minutes after Shirley had entered the building, wearing a dark blue suit with a rose in his lapel. Approximately 14 minutes later, the couple emerged from the building arm in arm. According to the report in the *South Wales Echo*, 'a group of housewives with prams, shopping in the busy street wished her, "Good luck, Shirley".'

When asked why she had chosen Hume, Shirley would later explain: 'He made me laugh, he was incredibly romantic and he asked me six times. I was crazy about the man.' But the more he saw of him, the more Sullivan came to loathe Hume, whom he thought 'pathetic.' Hume had ambitions of becoming a film producer. He had his own offices in London's Wardour Street, and employed several staff – but he was widely described as being a 'wheeler-dealer' type, and it's unclear how many of his creative projects ever actually came to fruition. Sullivan's suspicions that Hume had simply married Shirley for her money were deepened when the couple asked for Shirley's earnings to be paid into Hume's company account from then on. It also seemed to Sullivan that Hume was becoming unnecessarily involved in Shirley's career; Hume in turn began to snipe at Sullivan, suggesting that he should be waiting in the wings at each of Shirley's performances, to give her water and tissues whenever she needed them. 'My response to his demand that I become Shirley's skivvy was just two words. The second of them was "off".' It was obvious to everybody that this situation could not go on much longer. Then, while Shirley was appearing at Blackpool Opera House, Sullivan received a letter from Hume informing him that he was in breach of his contract with Shirley. Furious, Sullivan immediately travelled north, and confronted Hume in Shirley's dressing room. They argued about many things, and when Hume informed Sullivan that he did not want Sullivan to accompany them when Shirley appeared in New York later that year, for Sullivan it was the final straw. He told Hume that he could no longer stand for 'any more of this aggravation from you', and suggested that Hume buy him out from his contract with Shirley. If this was a bluff, Hume called it, and Sullivan was given a cheque for £10,000 as full settlement for his services (the equivalent of just under £350,000 today).

And that was that. But according to Sullivan, one evening shortly after he officially ceased to be Shirley's manager, he received a phone call from her. She was 'hysterical and distraught', because she had just discovered Hume in bed with their male chauffeur. Sullivan told her to come to him immediately, and soon afterwards she 'almost fell out of the taxi that stopped outside my flat. She was in a terrible state, screaming, sobbing and shaking, and I took her in and tried to comfort her. It was no good telling her, "I told you so", all I could do was cuddle her and let her pour her heart out to me.' Shirley told him that she'd really believed that she'd changed Hume, and that he 'was out of all that.' Before Sullivan could make any comment, Kenneth Hume also arrived at his door. He too was in tears, and Sullivan was now confronted by 'two weeping people, both trying to use me as a sounding board and peacemaker.'

Sullivan sent Shirley back home by taxi, while he gave Hume a serious talking-to. In spite of all their troubles, he told Hume, he still loved Shirley 'like a daughter' and would always be on call for her if she needed him – and if she needed him because Kenneth Hume was causing her more trouble, 'I will break your fucking neck, understand?' The weeping Hume could only nod. Sullivan told Hume to go home, that he would call Shirley and tell her to give her husband a second chance. He felt it was the only thing he could have done in the circumstances, since any other course of action would have made him look vindictive – but if Sullivan thought he was acting for the best, he also still seriously doubted that this marriage could actually work.

Sullivan later stated that he was convinced that at the time of 'the incident with the chauffeur' he could easily have wooed Shirley back as his client for a third time, but that for the sake of his health he decided against it. Enough was enough: 'I could not risk having Shirley Bassey as part of my life again.'

*

Michael Sullivan returned to working as an agent, and became a director of the Bernard Delfont agency. He began to specialize in handling comedians, and went on to represent Sid James, Eric Sykes, Mike and Bernie Winters, Dick Emery, Des O'Connor and many others. He and Shirley did not meet again until the early 1980s, when they bumped into each other at a party in Marbella in Spain hosted by Shirley's friend Soraya Khashoggi. According to Muriel Burgess, Shirley went up to Sullivan and embraced him saying, 'Hello, Mikey, it's good to see you.'

But in 1994, when Sullivan and his fifth wife Dany attended a concert of Shirley's at the Royal Festival Hall, they were refused entry backstage. Sullivan was then 74 years old, partially paralysed and in a wheelchair. Of course, it's always possible that Shirley simply never received the message that the Sullivans were waiting to see her (those who 'protect' the famous are not always competent); however, it's equally possible that she had been angered by

Sullivan's autobiography (which had been published 10 years earlier).

Sullivan's account of his years as Shirley's manager had tended to paint him as the hero of the story, although he did also vividly outline all his own faults, as well as Shirley's. Virtually all of the character defects he depicted in the Shirley he knew could be put down simply to her extreme youth at the time of their alliance; even so, perhaps Shirley never forgave him for the book, for she and Sullivan never spoke again. Sullivan and his wife both died during a fire at their Paris home in 1995.

Would Shirley Bassey have been a success without the help of Michael Sullivan? It's hard to say. If he hadn't called her up to London for an audition, she would probably have remained a waitress in Cardiff, and raised little Sharon. But it's hard to imagine her being content with that simple life forever; sooner or later she would probably have started singing again, and may well have eventually gotten a break in her career. If so, she would almost certainly have found herself a manager, perhaps even one who could coach and groom her as effectively as Sullivan did. Of course, the longer it took for all this to happen, the harder Shirley might then have found it to leave Sharon behind . . .

We will never know, but – for all his evident faults – Michael Sullivan's departure was still probably Shirley's loss. Her next two managers would also be her husbands, and both relationships were extremely complicated; the fact that both marriages failed is undoubtedly linked to the dual role her husbands played, which inevitably affected Shirley's feelings for them – and affected her career as well. In the light of this, it's entirely possible that Michael

Sullivan may well have been the best manager that Shirley Bassey would ever have.

*

With Sullivan out of the picture, Kenneth Hume now assumed the mantle of Shirley's manager himself. He booked her concert dates, dealt with her record company and the press, and invested her earnings. But he did not accompany her when she went on tour, although he did pay her the occasional visit while she was on the road. Instead, he made sure that Shirley always had a companion when she travelled, and her flights and hotels were always organized to perfection by his assistant Leslie Simmons. Shirley's travel pace certainly didn't slow down much after her marriage, despite the fact that in April she had undergone an operation to remove her tonsils; supposedly, she had been planning to embark on a dramatic project as an actress, but this illness had caused it to fall through. Although the operation was a success, during that summer she suffered badly from catarrh and nasal blockages, and was forced to cancel several shows as a result. Even so, in 1961 she still managed to tour the USA, played the Tivoli Gardens in Stockholm, and nightclubs in Antwerp, Brussels, Monte Carlo and the South of France.

If Shirley or her record company had any fears that her marriage might affect her popularity, they proved unfounded. 'I can only suppose it's because most of the record-buyers are girls,' Shirley observed at the time. 'The majority of my fan letters certainly are from girls.'

She and her husband undoubtedly made a strange couple. She was nocturnal, and he was not. They lived apart, with Kenneth maintaining his old bachelor flat in Bayswater, while Shirley had now bought a large house in Belgravia's Chester Square, and had installed a butler and a nanny there. Now that she was married, Shirley had reclaimed Sharon from her sister's care, and the little girl was now officially named Sharon Hume.

The Humes seldom – if ever – dined together. She liked fine food and champagne, and enjoyed breakfasting in bed on scrambled eggs. Kenneth Hume seemingly didn't drink alcohol at all, but consumed copious amounts of tea instead; he also chain-smoked 60 cigarettes a day and existed largely on a diet of junk food. As to whether the Humes slept together, one can only speculate. It would seem that at first both parties did try to make their marriage work (though not necessarily at the same time), but within two years their relationship had become an open marriage, and Hume's role in Shirley's life had become far more one of manager than husband.

Shirley's singles in 1961 included 'You'll Never Know', 'I'll Get By' and 'Reach For The Stars' backed with 'Climb Every Mountain'. This song from *The Sound of Music* soon stopped being merely a B-side, and eventually went to number one in the charts. Shirley was amazed that the record was a hit, 'as we were so late recording it' (*The Sound of Music* had first opened as a stage musical on Broadway in 1959). She brings to her version of the song the same kind of reverence that would mark her versions of both Bach's 'Ave Maria' and 'You'll Never Walk Alone', which were released the following year. 'You'll Never Walk Alone' originally came from the musical *Carousel*, and Shirley chose to cover the song well over a year before Gerry and the Pacemakers had a hit with it.

In September 1961, while Shirley was being interviewed by the *NME*'s Derek Johnson, the subject of her acting ambitions came up, and Kenneth Hume interjected: 'I honestly believe the general public will be very pleasantly surprised by Shirley's acting ability,' and promised that they would see proof of this 'within a year.' Referred to elsewhere as a 'musical comedy', whatever this project was remains unknown, although Hume and Shirley would continue to search for a stage vehicle for her for some years to come. Later that month Shirley toured the USA, making appearances at the Persian Room of New York's Plaza Hotel and in Las Vegas; in November she was back in Britain to headline on *Sunday Night at The London Palladium*, also appearing on the first Royal Variety Performance.

In January or February 1962, in what had now become her annual routine, Shirley returned to Australia. Apart from the pleasant climate and her popularity in the country, there were also two men there that she liked: Bruce Gordon in Sydney and John McAuliffe in Melbourne. At this point it's possible that Shirley may well still have been faithful to Kenneth Hume; within a year, that would have changed.

In April, Shirley spent two weeks appearing in variety at the London Palladium (where her support acts included Mike and Bernie Winters, Ted Rogers and Lionel Blair); she then set off on a 10-date tour of the UK with Nelson Riddle and his orchestra. Riddle was then Frank Sinatra's classic orchestral arranger, and Shirley wasn't about to pass up the chance to record an album with him herself. There were scheduling problems to overcome, plus the fact that Riddle was legally contracted to another record label, but

EMI's Norman Newell managed to overcome all these obstacles, and Riddle and Shirley entered the recording studio together shortly after their tour ended. The resulting album, *Let's Face The Music*, was largely a collection of standards with one absolutely standout track: 'What Now My Love.'

This was originally a French song by Gilbert Bécaud entitled 'Et Maintenant', and Riddle had originally said that he couldn't arrange it for Shirley, since he'd already done an arrangement of it for Sinatra. Norman Newell told Riddle that this was fine, they'd simply use another arranger for that track – but Riddle was so upset by the prospect of another arranger working on 'his' record that he stayed up all night before the recording session working on a *new* arrangement of the song, which he only completed a matter of hours before recording started, with parts of the orchestral score only reaching the studio halfway through the session. With its military drumming and a strident bass propelling the song along, Riddle's arrangement owed more than a passing debt to Ravel's *Bolero*. The album reached number 12 in the charts; 'What Now My Love' was released as the single, and went to number five.

In December, Shirley returned to the Persian Room of New York's Plaza Hotel, where she made a big impression on one particular member of the audience – Jackie Kennedy. The First Lady obviously had a word with her husband, because in January 1963 Shirley was one of the artists chosen to perform before President Kennedy as part of the celebrations for the second anniversary of his inauguration (confusingly, Shirley has always referred to this event as the 'inauguration party', which had actually taken place two years earlier). Suddenly discovering that she'd need an outfit other than her stage costume in which to meet the President after the concert, Shirley made a hurried shopping trip to the Nieman Marcus department store in Washington, where she bought a pink chiffon dress. It was styled very much like the famous white dress worn by Marilyn Monroe in *The Seven Year Itch*, and thus presumably appealed to JFK. When Shirley was introduced to the President after the show, she later described it as being 'one of the most exciting moments in my career.'

During the celebration concert Shirley had performed 'The Nearness of You', and 'Everything's Coming Up Roses' from the musical *Gypsy*, and was surprised to hear some of the audience laughing during the latter number, later admitting that she 'thought one of my boobs had come out.' It was only at the after-show party that she discovered the real reason for the laughter, when President Kennedy explained to her that the number had been Vice-President Lyndon Johnson's campaign song during the months leading up to the election.

Following the party, the President and all the performers were taken by motorcade to another informal event, at Vice-President Johnson's house. Here Shirley was horrified to discover that she was supposed to take part in some impromptu harmonizing with all the other singers, and was so 'terrified' that she hid under a table instead. Regardless, for Shirley, actually meeting Kennedy face to face was an intensely memorable experience: 'When I shook hands with him it was the weirdest experience in the world. Something shot right up my arm like an electric shock. I realized that I was shaking hands with the man who had the most power in the whole world.' Ten months later, Kennedy was assassinated in Dallas.

*

Shirley's next stop was Australia again, and this time her stay there would have a dramatic impact upon her life. When she returned to Britain two months later, she announced that she was pregnant. 'I'm pleased, although a little baffled,' Kenneth Hume told reporters at the time. 'Baffled' was probably an understatement, and Hume must at least have suspected that he couldn't be the child's father, and he might even have known it for certain. When he eventually sued Shirley for divorce, Hume categorically denied paternity, and had taken a blood test to prove it; what's more, one of the two men he named in his divorce petition was the Australian John McAuliffe. But that would not come about for nearly two more years.

At Easter-time Shirley returned to London's Palladium, where her support act was Matt Monro; this may have been the first date of a UK tour that Shirley undertook with Monro, and also with John Barry and his orchestra. In the late 1950s and early 1960s, the John Barry Seven had been, after the Shadows, the second most successful rock-and-roll instrumental group in the country. In 1959, Barry was also the musical director of Jack Good's influential pop TV show *Oh Boy*. After this he went on to arrange a string of hit records for the singer Adam Faith, in the course of which Barry developed his own inimitable orchestral sound. This led to him contributing music to Faith's debut film, *Beat Girl*, which led to more work soundtracks for several other B-movies – and then to James Bond. In the first Bond film *Dr No*, Barry's arrangement of

Monty Norman's 'The James Bond Theme' blended rock and jazz elements and was an instant Top 40 hit, spending three months in the charts. This immediately led to more high-profile film work for him, including the scores for *The L-Shaped Room*, *Zulu* and the second Bond film, *From Russia With Love*.

On the 1963 Shirley Bassey/Matt Monro tour, Barry went along as musical director and also played for the first half of the evening with his orchestra, the highlight being 'The Bond Theme'; in the second half Barry's orchestra backed Monro (who had his own Bond connection, as the singer of 'From Russia With Love') and Shirley. While on the road, Barry and Bassey are said to have enjoyed a brief affair. Although the romance didn't last, the two would shortly be reunited creatively, with dramatic results for both of them.

Shirley's most memorable release that was year was 'I (Who Have Nothing)', which was originally an Italian song called 'Uno Dei Tanti'; Shirley would also later record the song in Spanish as 'Hoy No Tengo Nada'. In any language, there were some who refused to believe that Shirley had nothing; that year America's *Ebony* magazine called her 'Britain's highest-paid entertainer', and claimed that she earned '$350,000-a-year.' This would have been around £120,000 at the time (or nearly £4 million today), and is almost certainly an overestimate.

At the time Shirley probably had other matters on her mind anyway. In November, her second daughter, Samantha Hume, was born in the London Clinic in Harley Street. Few people could seriously believe that Kenneth Hume had really fathered a baby, and privately there was much speculation as to who Samantha's real father might be. As with her first daughter, Shirley wasn't saying.

n i n e

THE MIDAS TOUCH

Having worked on the incidental music for the first two James Bond films (including adding his own powerful arrangement to the famous '007' theme), John Barry had badgered the Bond producers until they finally agreed to let him write a title song for the third film, *Goldfinger*. At this point the Bond franchise was nowhere near as big as it would later become, nor was recording a Bond theme an obviously beneficial career break for a singer. The first Bond film, *Dr No*, had had no theme song at all, and Matt Monro's rendition of Lionel Bart's theme for *From Russia With Love* had been only a minor hit in Britain.

Goldfinger was the film that would change all that, establishing Bond as a massive commercial property from that point on, and a global phenomenon. The film captured the public imagination, thanks to its gadget-laden Aston Martin, its laser-wielding villain and the unforgettable image of a naked Shirley Eaton covered in gold paint. It also probably helped that its theme song became a massive international hit – and for Shirley Bassey it would be one of the finest moments of her career. The fact that Shirley was a key part of the film's success may well have been a factor in her being asked to record two more Bond themes during the 1970s – and she remains the only artist ever to record more than one.

John Barry wrote the tune for 'Goldfinger' during early 1964, working on it night after night in his Cadogan Square flat until he was finally satisfied (and in the process keeping his houseguest Michael Caine awake). He played the tune to his regular lyricist, Trevor Peacock, with whom he'd written several hits for Adam Faith – but a week later Peacock admitted that he was stymied, and was unable to come up with anything suitable. Meanwhile, Barry had remained in touch with Shirley Bassey after their tour together the previous year. Although he knew that she had a firm policy of not listening to new songs before the lyrics were completed, one day Barry asked her to relax her rule and listen to the new tune he was working on. He told her that he hoped it would be the theme for the next James Bond film, and that he wanted her to sing it. Shirley agreed to listen to the tune as it stood and, as she later put it: 'Thank God I did, because the moment he played the music to me, I got goose pimples, and I told him, "I don't care what the words are, I'll do it".'

A year or so earlier, Barry had been instrumental in helping Anthony Newley and Leslie Bricusse to get *Fool Britannia*, their comedy LP collaboration with Peter Sellers, released. Perhaps feeling that they owed him a favour, Barry now approached the duo – who were at this point riding high on the success of their hit musical *Stop the World – I Want to Get Off* – and asked them to try and come up with something for the 'Goldfinger' lyrics. (Coincidentally, Shirley had recorded *Stop the World*'s 'What Kind of Fool Am I?' the year before, and was just about to score another minor hit with 'Who Can I Turn To' from another Newley/Bricusse musical, *The Roar of the Greasepaint – The Smell of the Crowd*).

When Newley and Bricusse visited John Barry at his London home, the composer played them his 'Goldfinger' tune – but on hearing the opening chords, Newley and Bricusse both spontaneously began singing the Mancini/Mercer hit from *Breakfast At Tiffany's*, 'Moon River', since the openings to both songs seemed identical to them. 'No, no! It's harmonically different,' Barry insisted. When they asked him what he thought the lyrics should be about, Barry responded, 'It's "Mack The Knife".' By that, he later explained, he'd meant to convey that 'it's a song about a bad guy, and there aren't that many songs about bad guys. "Mack The Knife" was the greatest one, set in that German period in the 1930s. So I said to them, "This is a guy – a villain – who paints women gold. It's pretty mad." And then they knew.'

It still wasn't easy. 'It nearly drove us crazy,' Newley admitted later. 'It took us weeks, because it wasn't a very long song, and you had to get all this information into a very short musical time span. But in the end I think it was one of the strongest lyrics we did. It's quite hard and informative, and it seems to hit right on the money as to who Goldfinger was.' Leslie Bricusse also explained that, 'The same way the films had those throwaway Bond one-liners with those puns, the songs all needed to have equally tongue-in-cheek lyrics, so that's what we did. I thought it was the silliest lyric I ever wrote.' After hearing Newley's demo of the song, Barry decided to add brass lines to his arrangement during an early screening of the film's credit sequence.

Barry was ecstatic when the Bond producers approved his choice of Shirley Bassey as the song's singer (which was almost certainly due to them being impressed by her star status). 'Choosing the singer was like casting a movie,' Barry later stated. 'It had to be the right choice. Shirley was great casting for "Goldfinger." Nobody could have sung it like her. She had that great dramatic sense. When it came to the studio, she didn't know what the hell the song was about, but she sang it with such total conviction that she convinced the rest of the world.'

It wasn't all plain sailing though, and the session's engineer Eric Tomlinson recalls Shirley being less than happy when the perfectionist Barry insisted on her recording take after take until he was absolutely satisfied, and her telling him so in no uncertain terms. 'She was certainly quite an outspoken lady,' Tomlinson observed with some understatement. Shirley herself would later complain about the length that Barry made her sustain one note, without any prior warning: 'I had to hold the note until I was blue in the face. They showed me the film, and I was singing to the credits.' She's also commented that – strangely – she's never had any further trouble sustaining that note ever since that day. According to Joan Collins, she and her then-husband Anthony Newley were both present in the control booth to watch the recording session.

With its Wagnerian chords, soaring strings and lyrical wit, delivered by Shirley's razor-sharp and crystal-clear vocal, 'Goldfinger' was a smash from the moment of its release. You couldn't really imagine anyone else singing it, either, although many other versions were recorded within weeks of its release, including one by Anthony Newley himself. But his co-writer Leslie Bricusse felt that Bassey's version of the song was definitive, simply because she 'sang its brains out.' Bricusse also went on to co-write another Bond theme with Barry, for *You Only Live Twice* (sung for the film by Nancy Sinatra, but Shirley would also record a version). Not everyone liked 'Goldfinger', though. One of the Bond producers, Harry Saltzman, absolutely hated the song, and would have voted for its removal if there had been enough time in their schedule to permit it; even after the song became a hit, he only grudgingly admitted that it worked.

As for the film's star, Shirley had known Sean Connery before he was even cast as Bond. 'I met Sean because I was the mascot for a showbiz 11 football team – I would go round with them and kick off the ball at the start of the match. I was lucky for them so they adopted me – and I was the only girl travelling with all these handsome showbiz people.' Though she's denied ever having had any romantic involvement with Connery herself, she's also admitted to being well aware of his charms: 'When he was Bond he was just *so* sexy. Those eyes. And that mouth; he was just sort of wickedly sexy. Whoa! And he was the best Bond, too.'

Shirley sang 'Goldfinger' live on stage at the Empire Leicester Square for the film's London premiere in September 1964. Although the record only reached number 21 in the British charts, it sold a million copies in the USA, where the film itself had just become the fastest-grossing release of all time. It might have sold even more copies, had Shirley been able to promote it in person – but she was touring Australia at the time, and was unable to break her contract there. Regardless, the song became (and remains) Shirley's biggest American hit, and her only top 40 US chart entry (it reached number eight). As a result of this, as soon as she was free to do so, she made appearances on the US chat shows hosted by Johnny Carson and Mike Douglas, which brought her to the attention of a much larger audience. 'Goldfinger' is also said to be the song that most inspired rock singer Alice Cooper to become a performer, and despite that dubious achievement the song is due to be inducted into the Grammy Hall of Fame in 2008.

*

Auric Goldfinger and James Bond were not the only new men to enter Shirley's life during 1964. In March of that year she had met the actor Peter Finch, who was then appearing on the London stage in a production of *The Seagull*. This was a brief return to the stage for the actor, who had started his career in British theatre before becoming a film actor in his late twenties. As a result of his appearance in such films as *A Town Like Alice* and *The Trials of Oscar Wilde*, by the 1960s Peter Finch had become an international star.

By anyone's standards, Finch had lived an extraordinary life. He was born in Britain, and when he was two years old, his parents divorced and for the rest of his childhood he was raised by his grandmother in France and India (where he met the young Krishnamurti and was tutored in spiritual matters by a Buddhist monk). When he was 10 years old his grandmother took him to Australia, where he worked at all manner of strange jobs before eventually becoming an actor – and in due course, an incorrigible womanizer and a heavy drinker.

During *The Seagull*'s London run, Finch's second wife Yolande and their two young children remained at the family home in Mill Hill, while he took a central London apartment at the Carlton

Towers in Sloane Street – in short, an ideal scenario in which to conduct an affair. Finch was immediately smitten with Shirley, and despite the fact that he was over 20 years older than her, the two were soon virtually inseparable. According to Muriel Burgess, Finch called Shirley 'Cheetah' (because of the way she walked) and she called him 'Finchy.' It seemed that Shirley was equally loves-truck, something confirmed by her later comment: 'My love affair with Finchy was a thing of great passion. He was so handsome and knowledgeable, I could curl up and listen to him for hours.' After all her disappointments in love, it seemed she believed that she had finally found, 'my knight in shining armour. The fairy story I never had. Here is the man who will give me all I have missed in life.'

The couple were not exactly discreet about their relationship, either. Shirley was then appearing at the Talk of the Town night-club, near Leicester Square, and Finch came to see her show every night after he had finished his own theatre performance. For her opening night at the venue, Shirley appeared on stage in a see-through white lace dress which Kenneth Hume had had Douglas Darnell design especially for her (the dress was later featured on the cover of Shirley's 1965 EP *Shirley Stops The Shows*). Unknown to Shirley, Hume arranged for a bright spotlight to be shone behind her when she made her entrance, thus revealing far more of her than she had anticipated. In fact, when she heard the sudden intake of breath from the audience, Shirley wondered (again) if she'd actually come out of the dress.

As for Kenneth Hume, Shirley's affair with Peter Finch made him insanely jealous. For the first time Shirley had taken a lover that could threaten his position; he could see that this wasn't just another casual fling, but a relationship that Shirley hoped had a long-term future to it. If his marriage to Shirley came to an end because of this, Hume probably feared that it would also mean the end of their business relationship – and he may have badly needed the income that Shirley generated, since it was rumoured that he had serious financial problems. These were said to be mainly gambling debts, and Hume supposedly owed a large amount of money to shady figures in London's gangland. Consequently, Hume wasn't about to just let Finch spirit Shirley away from him; he had a bad temper when roused, and during this period there were frequent rows in public between him and Shirley.

Shirley soon became convinced that she and Finch were being followed by private detectives hired by Hume, presumably to gather proof of her adultery in preparation for a divorce trial. But although this led Shirley to distrust every waiter and hotel porter she encountered, it didn't prevent her from continuing the affair with Finch, and at one point she had more or less moved into his apartment at the Carlton Towers. Shirley presumably told Finch of her acting aspirations, because he also asked his agent to find a play that they could star in together. The agent made polite noises of interest, but the idea came to nothing.

Of course, the nation's press were also soon on the couple's trail. While on a two-week nightclub booking in Beirut, Shirley as good as admitted to English journalists the fact that her marriage was over, and anyone who had been paying attention to showbiz gossip would have a good idea as to the reasons why. Returning to Britain in July for another *Night of a Hundred Stars* event at the Palladium, Shirley followed her heroine Judy Garland on the bill;

when Shirley had finished singing, Noël Coward – who was closing the show – pondered aloud, 'How the hell do you follow that?' Shirley and Coward became friends, and he was her escort to the premiere of *Goldfinger* two months later.

*

Meanwhile, Finch's wife Yolande was holidaying with their children in Italy when English reporters turned up on her doorstep and asked her how she felt about 'her husband's close friendship with Shirley Bassey.' When Peter Finch joined his wife in Italy shortly afterwards she confronted him regarding the affair, which he admitted, begging Yolande to 'let him get it out of his system.' That night Yolande accidentally took an overdose of sleeping pills, and was rushed to hospital; when she awoke there the next day she told her husband that she was going to divorce him.

This may well have raised doubts in Shirley's mind about Finch's worth as a person – and she was doubtless also aware that he had a serious problem with alcohol. Added to these drawbacks was the fact that he seemingly wanted her to completely give up her career and live her life in his shadow, which she was not prepared to do; in short, she began to seriously doubt Finch's ability to give her all she 'had missed in life' after all. In August, Finch travelled to Israel to film *Judith* with co-star Sophia Loren. The film itself was a farcical disaster, and although Shirley flew to Israel to join Finch on location, director Daniel Mann recalled there being 'great arguments' between the two. Peter Finch had asked Shirley to marry him, but she had turned him down; as a result, their relationship came to an abrupt end, and it hit him hard. Shirley later explained that, 'I think it had been a dream for him, a dream that could never have worked.' As Finch's biographer Trader Faulkner put it, Shirley had 'challenged him as an artist and fired him as a man. She was the only woman who threw Peter totally off balance by being every bit as good as him as an artist and by refusing to marry him and just leaving him.'

Finch took the rejection badly, and talked about Shirley endlessly to anyone who would listen. He claimed that he had suffered racist threats and attacks because of his relationship with her (including being sent a letter bomb, which fortunately didn't go off). Finch also complained that his career had suffered because of Shirley, that he had been boycotted by cinema chains in both South Africa and the Southern states of the USA (both areas where a mixed-race relationship would have caused outrage). But Finch still couldn't forget her. Later that year, while filming *The Flight of the Phoenix* in California, he called Shirley by phone and begged her to join him in Hollywood. She supposedly agreed, then afterwards began to waver; a few days later she cabled him to tell him her final answer: no. According to his friends, Finch wept for two days before eventually accepting the situation.

Muriel Burgess states that Finch and Shirley met again by chance in Switzerland three years later, when he was accompanied by a young Jamaican girl named Eletha. A few days later Finch called Shirley to tell her that he couldn't stand seeing her again, and was returning to Jamaica. It was the last time that they would ever meet. Finch and Eletha subsequently married, and the couple remained together until his death of a heart attack in 1977, at the age of 58. After parting from Shirley, Finch had gone on to have an extremely successful film career; he was nominated for an Oscar for his role in 1971's *Sunday Bloody Sunday*, and awarded one posthumously for his last major film, 1976's *Network*. Despite the pain of their break-up, Shirley evidently retained a large amount of fondness for Peter Finch; in recent years she has referred to him as 'an adorable man.'

Meanwhile, in February 1965, Yolande Finch began divorce proceedings on the grounds of her husband's admitted adultery with Shirley Bassey. Later the same month, the divorce court heard Kenneth Hume's petition against Shirley, citing her admitted affairs with Peter Finch and John McAuliffe. It was at this point that Hume also denied his paternity of Samantha, and suggested that one of these two men was actually the child's father (Mike Sullivan also seems to suggest that Shirley's affair with Finch pre-dates his arrival in London). Amazingly, although their marriage was at an end, Shirley still kept Kenneth Hume on as her manager. Perhaps it was a case of 'the devil you know.'

It was possibly in response to all this that Shirley chose to record an English-language version of the song made famous by Edith Piaf, 'Non Je Ne Regrette Rien' . . . or, as it was titled in English, 'No Regrets.'

THE ROSES

As her divorce case was being heard, Shirley went on the road again, travelling to Singapore (where she played a concert with Matt Monro), Australia and the USA. After some dates in Las Vegas, she travelled to Hollywood, where she was joined for some holiday time by her two daughters and their nanny. Kenneth Hume also briefly joined Shirley here, to organize her appearance on a couple of TV shows. The first of these was a guest slot on the *Dean Martin Show* (Dean and Shirley got on extremely well), and the second was a TV special in which she shared the spotlight with the legendary Count Basie (with whom relations were a little cooler). Basie was on an extremely tight schedule, as he was in the middle of a tour at the time; he flew in for one day to record his three numbers for the show, and then flew straight out again. The taping had all gone smoothly, but after Basie left the studio Shirley still had one last number to film. When she came down from her dressing room, dressed up and ready for the cameras, she discovered that the entire TV crew had just departed to take an unscheduled 20-minute break. Shirley's first reaction was to go ballistic, complaining loudly about how badly she was being

treated. Her musical director Kenny Clayton thought he detected
the influence of the highly theatrical Kenneth Hume in Shirley's
attitude, but fortunately she calmed down before any real damage
could be done to her relationship with the TV network. In 1994
Shirley admitted, 'I used to make terrible scenes because I thought
that was the way I had to act. Now I know better. I've learned how
to say, "Sorry".'

*

By the summer of 1965 Shirley had returned to the UK, and that
September – backed by the Alyn Ainsworth orchestra – she opened
for an eight-week season at London's Pigalle Theatre, at a record-
breaking salary of £3,000 per week (the equivalent of approximately
£83,000 a week today). Although the venue was also a restaurant,
Shirley absolutely refused to appear on stage until her audience
had finished eating and all the plates had been cleared away;
Shirley had had more than enough of being 'thrown in with the
dinner' in American clubs, and now that she was a much bigger
star, she saw no reason why she had to put up with it any more.
On her opening night at the Pigalle, Kenneth Hume pulled off a
publicity stunt worthy of Michael Sullivan's finest efforts, when he
persuaded Shirley to sing 'The Second Time Around' during her
set and dedicate it to the man she was going to marry – 'my
ex-husband, Kenneth Hume.' Naturally, her announcement
caused an audience uproar of support and congratulations. After
the show, reporters were invited backstage to admire the 1,000 red
roses that Hume had sent to Shirley, and her huge new diamond
engagement ring. Hume told the *South Wales Echo*, 'I didn't

propose to Shirley – I didn't need to. We are both so much in love and I think we always have been.' He also stated that they hadn't yet set a date for the wedding, but they would of course let the press know when they did. Photos of the couple embracing made the front pages of numerous papers the following morning.

Was all this simply a publicity stunt? Probably, since Shirley Bassey's second marriage to Kenneth Hume never took place. She continued to wear the engagement ring, but deftly changed the subject whenever anyone asked when she was actually getting married. After six months or so, she finally told reporters that there had been a change of plans and that, 'We've decided against re-marrying. We're much better friends as we are.' In retrospect, it seems incredibly unlikely that Shirley ever seriously contemplated going through with a second marriage to Kenneth Hume, although it must remain a possibility.

One night at the Pigalle, Shirley came close to losing her voice on stage because she had been crying beforehand ('It is fatal, because your voice box closes up'). About to leave for the theatre, she had gone up to the nursery to spend a few moments with little Samantha, 'and she was so independent, doing her own thing, and I was trying to play with her and she was, "No, no, no." And she was only three! She didn't want to know and I couldn't stop crying. I was in a terrible state.' A doctor at the theatre gave Shirley a tranquillizer, 'but it left my nerves dead and you need your nerves. You need the adrenalin. If the adrenalin doesn't flow, the nerves take over. Your hands go like this [Shirley displayed her exaggeratedly shaking hands]. After that, I took to sipping cognac before I went on. I developed a taste later for champagne instead.'

Regardless, Shirley's run at the Pigalle was a huge success, and the *Melody Maker* review of the show called her 'Britain's number one cabaret attraction.' Her last album release for EMI/Columbia Records was *Shirley Bassey At The Pigalle*, recorded live during the course of her run. Her final single releases for the label had been fairly unremarkable, but included one song that had obviously been given her simply because of 'Goldfinger'. This was the theme for *The Liquidator*, a spoof spy thriller in the Bond mould; its title song is undeniably influenced by 'Goldfinger' but nowhere near as good, and it's a measure of Shirley's talent that she was able to sing its rather weak lyric with as much conviction as she did.

Around this time Shirley auditioned for a role in Lionel Bart's new musical about Robin Hood, *Twang!* She failed to get the part, but since the show itself closed almost immediately after it opened, Shirley wasn't too disappointed. She was more upset when told that she wouldn't be playing Nancy in the film version of *Oliver!*, which was also decided during this period. Even though the director Sir Carol Reed apparently wanted Shirley to play the part, the film's producers felt that if a coloured actress took the role it would by definition have made the film much more racially sensitive, given that Nancy is battered to death by a white man (Bill Sykes, played brilliantly in the film by Oliver Reed, the nephew of the director).

One Sunday in November 1965 Shirley began filming her own BBC TV Special, *The Sounds of Shirley Bassey* – the first time she had ever had a TV show devoted entirely to her. During rehearsals for the show Shirley had a shouting match with Kenneth Hume about the inclusion of one number in which she had to dance as well as sing; during the argument Shirley fainted, and was admitted to the London Clinic for a few days' rest, after which filming was completed. The TV show wasn't broadcast until nearly a year later, in August 1966.

Shirley's recording contract with EMI had now expired, and rather than renew it Kenneth Hume negotiated a new contract with United Artists (a company so-called because it had originally been founded – as a film company – by Douglas Fairbanks Jr, Mary Pickford and Charlie Chaplin). Although Shirley would have preferred to continue recording in Britain, she was now spending much more time in the USA, and being signed to an American label would make it much easier to record there.

*

In January 1966, Shirley had her twenty-ninth birthday, and since she hated the idea of turning 30 the following year, she announced her intention to 'stay 29 for ever.' That month she flew to Australia (as was now her usual practice at that time of year), but this time she was accompanied by her two daughters – plus her musical director Kenny Clayton and a new road manager, her ex-lover Bernard Hall (who had been hired by Hume, who also knew him). Shirley was delighted that her daughters could now accompany her on the road, saying, 'It's wonderful to take my children all over the world with me.' But it wasn't always easy, especially when they were all stuck in foreign airports because of flight delays – and the girls could only stay with Shirley for six weeks. After that, they returned to England with their nanny, because Sharon had to start school. As would always happen at the end of school holidays, Shirley found that 'the hardest thing of all was saying goodbye to my girls.'

In Melbourne she endured a terrible booking that had been arranged by Kenneth Hume through John McAuliffe (strangely, since McAuliffe had been named by Hume as a co-respondent in his divorce petition). The venue was the Roaring Twenties nightclub, which had recently been converted from an old chocolate factory, and still smelled of chocolate. The building was little more than a large shed with a corrugated roof, which had no ventilation or air conditioning, and no separate bathroom or toilet for Shirley to use. When she rang Hume in London to complain about being booked into such a shoddy dump and tell him about the appalling working conditions she was having to put up with, Hume was extremely unsympathetic, dismissing her grievances as mere fussiness; she became so angry that she slammed the phone down on him. Rather than walk out of the booking, Shirley suffered through it as best she could, but during this period she and Bernard Hall briefly became lovers again.

Sydney – where she played a month-long residency at a club called Chequers – was much better, and the *Sydney Sunday Telegraph* called her 'sinuous, tempestuous, with a voice that raises the roof.' But this tour of Australia had been soured for Shirley, not just by the Melbourne booking but also by the posters she saw at airports which outlined the country's racist new immigration policy: 'Keep Australia White.'

*

Shirley's Sydney agent Charlie Baxter accompanied the party on to New Zealand, where he and Shirley became lovers (the Hall affair having come to a natural end) and she performed under terrible conditions because of a flood. At least she couldn't blame that on Hume, but the next booking was definitely his fault, and as bad – or worse – than the chocolate factory. En route to the USA they had a three-day stopover in the Philippines, and Hume had booked Shirley a one-night show at the Nile Club in Manila. This turned out to be a tiny bar, whose resident band could barely speak English and couldn't read sheet music. Kenny Clayton had to scour the city to find a handful of musicians that he could work with, while Shirley spent as much time on her hair and costume as she would have done for any prestige booking – but when showtime came round the bar was still virtually empty, apart from a small group of its regular clientele. Shirley sang just three songs before giving it up as a bad job. The fact that Kenneth Hume had booked her into two such terrible venues in quick succession indicates either managerial incompetence on his part for booking venues sight unseen, or else perhaps that he was exacting some form of petty revenge on Shirley for the Finch affair. Or both. The fact that Shirley was able to kiss and make up with Hume after incidents like this speaks volumes of the depth of their relationship, but is also a mystery to most observers. Hume was widely disliked in the business, and Shirley's mother Eliza once stated: 'I could never get on with Kenneth Hume. I couldn't even talk to him.' On another occasion she was even more candid: 'I couldn't stand the man.'

*

Arriving in the USA in April, Shirley next appeared in cabaret at the Sahara Hotel in Las Vegas, performing two shows a night, seven nights a week for six weeks. While there, she reportedly had another affair, with a French dancer friend of Hall's named Rudolph. She then moved on to New York, where she played a season at the Royal Box nightclub in the Americana Hotel; she also had to consult a throat specialist in New York, possibly because her voice had been affected by the desert air. But the primary purpose of her visit to the city was to record her first session for her new record label, and she had a preliminary meeting with musical arranger Ralph Burns (who had worked with Woody Herman, Lena Horne, Sarah Vaughan and Barbra Streisand, among others) to choose and rehearse material prior to rehearsals and recording. The resulting album, *I've Got A Song For You*, was recorded over a one-week period, but is a bit of a musical mish-mash, consisting mainly of cover versions. Even so, Shirley would soon reinvent herself again artistically on United Artists, although she later stated that when she had signed with the label, 'my voice was changing just like the new material. I didn't consciously attempt to change the way I sang, it was more of a natural development. I recorded the early United Artists albums in the USA, but I didn't particularly enjoy the experience of doing them there. I was much happier recording in the UK.'

That summer she returned to Britain, and in July she headlined her own show, *Shirley Bassey Entertains*, at London's Prince of Wales Theatre. In August she released a single, 'Don't Take The Lovers From The World', which she and Hume had high hopes for. To give the song some much needed TV exposure, she booked in to sing it to the nation on the *Eamonn Andrews Show*, which was broadcast live. During rehearsals for this show, Kenneth Hume complained repeatedly about the sound balance being wrong, that it was reproducing Shirley's vocal badly. He forced his way into the control room and insisted that he wanted to handle the sound mixing himself during the live broadcast. When the show's producer Malcolm Morris refused and asked him to leave, the argument became heated, with Hume swearing profusely; in the end, Morris called security guards and had Hume physically ejected from the building. By this point the show had started, and – unsure how all this would be resolved – Andrews even announced that Shirley would not be appearing after all, because of voice trouble. Somehow, the troubled waters were calmed, and Shirley's voice miraculously returned after the commercial break. But Hume's tantrum at the show gained widespread newspaper attention, which he only made worse by loudly sneering at the low fee Shirley had received for appearing on the show (£200), given that she had just signed a Las Vegas contract that would earn her more than £175,000 over a three-year period; in short, he had conveniently forgotten that her fee for the show was just a token gesture, since she was basically using her appearance just to promote her new record, and had in fact been desperate to do so. After this incident, Kenny Clayton – who had never got on with Hume – announced that he would never work with him again.

Shirley always saw more in Hume than anyone else could, as she told the *People*'s Arthur Helliwell: 'It seems that I had to get married then go through a divorce to really become mates with Kenneth, my manager. He's helped me a great deal about money. I've learned to save and invest.' But a new man was about to enter Shirley's world. On a brief visit to Venice for a gala appearance at the Hotel Excelsior, Shirley became friendly with one of the hotel's managers, an Italian named Sergio Novak, who would play a major role in her life during the decade to come.

Meanwhile, Kenneth Hume was making plans for Shirley to star in a London stage musical, which he announced would open in the autumn of 1967. This was to be *Josephine*, with Shirley taking the title role of the consort of the Emperor Napoleon (who had herself been a mixed-race Creole, from Martinique). There were those who thought Hume had chosen the subject matter because it echoed his own relationship with Shirley – that is, that he fancied himself as an emperor. Some sources claim that Lionel Bart had agreed to write the songs for the show, while others indicate that Kenneth Hume had signed up two unknown (and unnamed) song-writers instead. It was definitely intended that Anthony Newley should co-star as Napoleon, but, although plans were afoot for rehearsals to begin in early 1967, in the end Hume was unable to raise enough money for the show, and it failed to get off the ground (Newley supposedly attempted to revive plans for the show himself some years later, this time with Barbra Streisand as his co-star, but once again the concept stalled at the planning stage).

Then, in June 1967, Kenneth Hume died. He had had several illnesses that summer, including one bout of pneumonia; on another occasion, he had nearly died from an accidental overdose of sleeping pills. Hume took these pills regularly, because he suffered from depression-related insomnia (he was probably bipolar, or manic depressive, in fact, which might explain some of his odder behaviour). Hume's doctor was also concerned that he just wasn't eating enough. Hume's death was caused by another

overdose of sleeping pills, which would appear to have been accidental once again. It seems very unlikely to have been a suicide
attempt. There was no note, for one thing; nor had Hume ever
mentioned the possibility of suicide in relation to his own bouts of
depression. Also, the dosage he had taken was so small that it
would not have been fatal to any healthy person – but Kenneth
Hume was not a well man, and the post-mortem examination
discovered that, unknown to anyone, he had been suffering from
heart disease. The coroner's verdict was one of accidental death,
from what he termed an 'incautious overdose.'

Shirley was devastated by Hume's death. Despite everything they
had gone through, the couple had 'remained each other's best
friend. I was so angry with Kenneth for leaving me like that. How
could he do that to me? And why? I knew he was unhappy. And he
wasn't well; he suffered from emphysema. But I discovered afterwards that he'd been receiving electric shock treatment. I was so
angry with the doctors. I was screaming down the phone at them.'
Hume had presumably received the electric shock treatment
referred to as treatment for his depression.

At the time of Hume's death Shirley had been busily rehearsing
for a six-week season of cabaret, but grief overtook her and she took
to her bed. 'I was in a terrible state. I was about to open at the Talk
of the Town, and Bernard Delfont, who owned it, sent a message
saying that he knew what I was going through and that I should
cancel if I felt I wasn't up to it. He'd quite understand. No impresario had ever been so kind to me . . . Of course, it had the reverse
effect. The whole season was booked solid. I felt I couldn't let him
down.' She told the press, 'Kenneth would want me to carry on.'

So the show went on, even though opening night could not help but be a deeply emotional event. 'I sang a song with lyrics that seemed to be written especially for me and Kenneth. 'Goodbye,' I sang. 'This is where our story ends. Ever lovers, ever friends.' Somehow, I managed to get to the end and then half-ran, sobbing, into the wings. There was a nurse waiting and she stabbed me in the bottom with a needle. The audience was going mad. It was an emotional love-in. They knew what I was going through. They knew I'd buried Ken just a week before.'

Of course, it wasn't just grief that Shirley was feeling. There was guilt as well, and above all confusion. She had relied on this man for over six years. In spite of the jealousy, the arguments and the gambling debts, Kenneth Hume had always been there for her. Ironically, she had recently recorded a version of 'If You Go Away', a poignant song of loss the lyrics of which now seemed horribly appropriate. What was she going to do without him?

e l e v e n

THE ITALIAN

Shortly after Kenneth Hume's death, Shirley very nearly joined him. According to Muriel Burgess, during one insomniac night Shirley took sleeping pill after sleeping pill simply because she was unable to get any sleep, and in the course of this lost track of how many she had swallowed; at some point she realized that there was something very wrong, and managed to stumble along the corridor towards the bedroom of her secretary Jean Lincoln before collapsing. Lincoln somehow manoeuvred the woozy Shirley into her car and drove her straight to hospital; fortunately, they arrived in time, and all was subsequently well. Ironically, some time later Jean Lincoln herself died from an accidental overdose of sleeping pills; her death hit Shirley hard, as the two had been very close friends. She later commented, 'When she died I was so upset. She didn't mean to kill herself. I don't think I have ever allowed any woman to get that close to me again. I loved her.'

Filling the vacuum that Kenneth Hume had left in her life was easier than it might have been, as Hume's old assistant Leslie Simmons now took over managing all of Shirley's business affairs. Hume's will had divided his estate between Leslie Simmons, Shirley and his own relatives. Hume left a total of £11,286; this was surprisingly low for a man accustomed to driving limousines, but showed just how much his gambling habit had taken its toll.

As well as Simmons, on a personal level Shirley came to rely upon another close friend of Kenneth Hume's, Beaudoin Mills. An antiques dealer, in later years Mills would become Shirley's main aide-de-camp, and her regular escort to social events whenever she was between boyfriends; he was frequently referred to as her 'personal manager.'

Her life slowly began to return to normal, and towards the end of the summer of the hippies, Shirley Bassey was appearing in cabaret at the Empire Room of New York's Waldorf-Astoria Hotel. As was still often the case, she performed two shows per night, six days per week. The advertisement for the show promised: 'Dinner and supper are included, and there is continuous dancing to two orchestras.'

Her next album, *And We Were Lovers*, was released that autumn, and included numerous songs from movies and musicals. Sleeve notes were provided by the songwriter/poet Rod McKuen, whose 'If You Go Away' (an English-language version of Jacques Brel's 'Ne Me Quitte Pas') was included on the album. But the best-known track, and by far the biggest single hit, was 'Big Spender' from the Cy Coleman and Dorothy Fields musical *Sweet Charity*. In the show the song is sung as a come-on from dance-hall girls to prospective customers – and if it isn't actually blatantly sexual, it isn't very far from it, either. Perhaps that was its appeal for Shirley, who confessed to *FHM* magazine in 2000: 'I do think there's a frustrated stripper in me trying to get out. When I do "Big Spender", I'm away. I love doing that – I never get tired of it.' To compound the song's raunch-iness, Douglas Darnell had created a special gown for Shirley to wear while promoting it, with a thigh-high split that was even more revealing than usual. As Shirley later put it, 'I said to Doug, "What am I going to wear underneath?" And he said, "As little as possible".' In fact, as Shirley admitted in the 1990s, 'I rarely wear underwear on stage. It's been like that all my career. From the year dot my body has been sewn into my dresses.'

Shirley once described her favourite pastime as being 'shopping, shopping, shopping', so it's little surprise that she has a special soft spot for 'Big Spender', describing it as her 'favourite fun song': 'I'm a big spender. Money doesn't impress me, but it allows me to buy what I want and to help my family and friends.'

In a curious footnote, it was later accidentally discovered that Shirley's version of 'Big Spender' was highly effective at clearing pigeons from the runways at Liverpool airport when played at loud volume.

*

In early 1968, Shirley accepted a booking to appear in cabaret at the Hotel Excelsior in Venice. Part of the reason she accepted may well have been a desire to become reacquainted with the hotel's manager, Sergio Novak. However it happened, the two were soon deeply – and obviously – involved with each other. For once, she had chosen a man closer to her own age (she was 31 and he 34), and their whirlwind romance seemed to be working out. Of course, the press soon became aware of Sergio's existence, even if they managed to get his name wrong (the Welsh *Western Mail* announced that Shirley would soon be marrying an Italian named 'Roberto Vincento').

On 13 August 1968, Shirley Bassey married her second husband Sergio Novak, in a brief ceremony that took place at 2.30 in the morning. The venue was the Little Church of the West in Las Vegas (where Shirley was appearing in cabaret at the Sahara Hotel), and both of Shirley's daughters were bridesmaids. The bride wore blue, and in the wedding photographs she looks extremely happy, and very much in love (Sergio, on the other hand, looks rather wooden). 'My daughters adore Sergio,' Shirley told the press. 'He will be a wonderful father.' As time went by, this proved to be the case, and Shirley's daughters both took Novak's name.

Their family expanded very quickly. She and Sergio soon became the legal guardians of her niece's son, Mark Allen (the grandson of Shirley's sister Ella), whom they would eventually adopt as their own son. As Shirley later explained, 'My son is my great-nephew, and he was only 18 months old and he was going to end up in a children's home and I couldn't bear that.' Mark had been born with a digestive disorder called malabsorption, and his mother Barbara was unable to afford the expensive dietary treatment this illness required; when Shirley offered to take care of Mark, his mother was happy for her to do so.

During 1968, Shirley was reunited with John Barry for another film soundtrack. 'My Love Has Two Faces' was the title theme for a thriller called *Deadfall*, a Hitchcockian thriller starring Michael Caine. Unfortunately, the film was pretty dreadful and the tune less than inspiring; however, the Barry/Bassey alliance would have better moments in the coming years. Meanwhile, a Bond connection of sorts carried on with Shirley's LP *12 Of Those Songs*, which rather bizarrely featured sleeve notes by Sean Connery.

*

Before the year was over, Shirley became pregnant, much to Sergio's delight. Then, in January 1969 Shirley and Sergio travelled to Australia, where Shirley came down with a viral throat infection. She seemed to be recovering, but a week later she became suddenly ill during a performance, and was rushed to hospital; while there, she had a miscarriage. Understandably, the couple were deeply upset at the loss of their child, and the rest of her Australian tour was cancelled. Although the couple continued to try to conceive for many years, Shirley never became pregnant again.

Later that year Shirley and Sergio moved to Switzerland, settling in Lugano near the Italian border. For the first year or so they lived in a house in the town, but eventually built their own home there, Villa Capricorn (which Shirley later described as being 'right on the lake with a big swimming pool, grotto and a boat. It was really wonderful – a lovely, lovely villa'). Sharon was sent to a Swiss boarding school, while Samantha and Mark were looked after by the family's English nanny Thelma whenever Shirley was on tour. Shirley's move to Switzerland took place at least partly for tax purposes. This meant that she was unable to work in the UK for a period of two years, and was at least partly the reason why the albums *Does Anyone Miss Me* and *This Is My Life* were recorded mainly in Los Angeles. When she moved to Switzerland, Shirley inadvertently took more of her money out of the UK than she was entitled to under Treasury regulations. The mistake was eventually ironed out, with Shirley commenting, 'I innocently took money that was mine so I could start a new life.'

As for Sergio's new life, it gradually became more entwined with Shirley's career. He seemed able to cope with all the adulation his new wife attracted: 'My wife has thousands of male admirers who send her flowers and love letters. I accept this attention from her fans. But if someone flirts with her in front of me, my coolness disappears.' And he also seemed more than capable of dealing with Shirley's fiery temperament, stating, 'Shirley will argue with me and she can still blow her top. Shirley has had things all her way for the past few years. So I leave her alone, sometimes for eight hours, sometimes a day, then she comes to me and says what a good idea I had . . . and the argument is over.' As for Shirley, she seemed to accept that she had met her match, cheerfully joking, 'I'm going to make a real effort to learn Italian so that I shall be able to swear at Sergio in his own language.'

Whatever the dynamics of their relationship, it obviously made her happy: 'When I lived in Britain I was always Shirley Bassey and always on show. In Lugano I am Mrs Novak and just loaf around, casually dressed and without make-up – and nobody bothers. Sergio has made me contented and secure and it is about time I was. After all, I have been in show business since I was 17.' Sergio persuaded Shirley to relax more, and take more frequent holidays. The whole family went skiing in the Alps in the winter and to Italian beaches in the summer. This was a radical change of lifestyle for Shirley, who even started living a less nocturnal lifestyle: 'I love skiing. It's the only sport that I don't mind getting up at nine in the morning for.' She also took up tennis and water-skiing, and seemed to become much more relaxed.

Sergio had given up his work in hotel management, but he was not content to simply be a kept man, trailing around the planet in Shirley's wake. Very much a traditional Italian, Sergio wanted to feel like the dominant partner in their marriage ('That is what every woman wants, a home where the man is boss,' he told one reporter), or at the very least, on an equal footing with his wife. After Shirley left England, her affairs were managed by an English agent and manager named Robert Patterson; but as time went by and he learnt more about the ins and outs of show business, Sergio eventually took over the business side of things and became his wife's new manager.

In 1969 Shirley also performed at Italy's San Remo Song Festival, with a song she had recorded the year before. This was the Italian song 'La Vita', which became 'This Is My Life' in English. Although Shirley didn't reach the finals, there was a campaign of support for her in the Italian press, who thought she should have won. The song became something of a personal anthem for Shirley, and swiftly became established as the regular closing number of all her live performances .

Another key song came her way in 1970 when the Beatles released *Abbey Road*, their final studio album (the *Let It Be* album was actually recorded prior to that); and they went out on a high note, since the record was positively crammed with good tunes. For many, the standout track was George Harrison's 'Something'; Frank Sinatra went so far as to call it 'the greatest love song of the past 50 years', and it swiftly became one of the Beatles' most covered songs. One of the first people to do so was Peggy Lee, who sang it on the Ed Sullivan TV show; Shirley saw her singing it, and fell in love with the song: 'I just caught the end of Peggy's perform-ance. I was knocked out of my mind. I have to record that number, I told myself.' As observed previously, Shirley had a good ear for picking material, but when she announced that she wanted to cover this song she ran into some fierce opposition from her musical advisers: 'When I first sang it everybody said, "Oh, no, no, no." Then, when I wanted to record it, they said, "No, no, no, it's a Beatles song, it's a group song." And the more they told me not to do it, the more I wanted to. And when I did do it I proved them wrong, because it was number four in England for me.' The single was indeed a hit (as was the album – of the same title – which went to number five and was her biggest seller to date, selling over five million copies worldwide). In fact, Shirley delivered an extremely creditable version of the song (the same cannot be said, alas, for her subsequent version of the Beatles' 'Fool On The Hill', which was pretty awful).

The *Something* album was produced and arranged by Johnny Harris, and Shirley was backed on some of the sessions by the rock group Heads, Hands And Feet. Also included on the album were versions of other contemporary tunes: the Doors' 'Light My Fire', Blood, Sweat & Tears' 'Spinning Wheel', and 'Easy To Be Hard' from the musical *Hair*, alongside new 'standards' like 'My Way' and Michel Legrand's Oscar-nominated 'What Are You Doing the Rest of Your Life?' from the movie *The Happy Ending* (a song covered by numerous other artists, including Frank Sinatra and Dusty Springfield). The album showed a whole new dimension to Shirley as an artist, and brought her to the attention of a much wider audience; as she later commented, 'The recording of the

Something album was a major turning point for me. You could even say it made me a pop star.'

The photograph on *Something*'s album cover showed Shirley wearing one of Douglas Darnell's most daring creations: a citrus-yellow dress that featured paisley teardrop-shaped peepholes placed at strategic intervals (including one on a buttock) which revealed Shirley's bare skin showing through from underneath. She later described the dress as being 'sexy, without being over the top', and recounted how she'd worn it on stage a few years later, at the Empire Room of New York's Plaza Hotel. As she'd introduced the song 'I, Capricorn' with the comment 'I happen to be a Capricorn,' a voice in the audience called out, 'I'm a Capricorn too!' Peering into the crowd, Shirley discovered that the voice belonged to Ava Gardner ('looking gorgeous'), and promptly hitched up her dress and strode across the dining tables to go and say hello, her gaze defying the men in the audience to even *think* about trying to grab at her exposed flesh.

*

In the late summer of 1970 Shirley returned to Britain for the first time since her exile began, to play a two-week booking at London's Talk of the Town (which was also a record-breaking sell-out); she was joined on stage on her final night by the cast of the London production of *Hair* for a rendition of the show's anthem 'Aquarius'. One of her shows at the venue was recorded for the *Live at Talk of the Town* album, released soon after. Shirley returned to Britain in November for a 10-date tour that took in both London (£2.50 a ticket at the Royal Festival Hall) and Cardiff.

In April 1971 she returned yet again, for a concert at the Royal Albert Hall. Also that year – and at John Barry's insistence – Shirley recorded her second James Bond theme, 'Diamonds Are Forever'. Not only was the song a genuine classic and one of the very best Bond theme songs ever, but the film itself was also a return to form, with Sean Connery reprising his role as the secret agent after some years' absence. Even so, Bond producer Harry Saltzman once again hated the song, and especially Don Black's lyrics, which he thought vulgar and obvious; he was, once again, utterly wrong. John Barry refused to compromise or back down on the matter, and eventually won the day. Certainly Shirley herself could identify with the lyrics, as she once commented, 'Diamonds never leave you. Men do.' In 2005 Kanye West sampled the song for his hit 'Diamonds from Sierra Leone', which won the 2006 Grammy for 'Best Rap Song.'

Shirley's 1971 album *Something Else* was also produced and arranged by Johnny Harris, and made the Top Ten upon release. Once again it saw her covering more contemporary tunes, including 'Where Do I Begin' (the theme from *Love Story*) and Paul Simon's 'Bridge Over Troubled Water.' That November, Shirley was back in Britain again, to take part in the Royal Variety Performance at the Palladium. After the show, Shirley went to a restaurant with a friend and got into an argument with a waiter after receiving poor service; the argument escalated, and she ended up slapping him. On a lighter side, it was probably during this visit that Shirley filmed her fondly-remembered guest appearance on the *Morecambe and Wise Christmas Special,* which was broadcast on Christmas Day. The comedy duo were then at their creative peak, and A-list actors and celebrities were queuing up to allow Eric and Ernie to make fools of them. In 1971 their Christmas guests included Glenda Jackson and André Previn as well as Shirley.

In the show, Shirley enters with a bouffant hairdo, wearing a sparkling evening gown with a thigh-high split. Eric and Ernie gush about how glad they are to have her on the show, and Ernie promises her, 'We've built a special set for you.' There then follows a comedy routine (devised by the show's choreographer Ernest Maxin) in which Shirley performs 'Smoke Gets In Your Eyes' while Eric and Ernie, dressed as workmen in long brown coats, are caught out turning a huge handle that operates the revolving stage she is standing on. Shirley then makes her way off the stage down some steps – which prove to be incredibly shoddily made, as the heel of Shirley's slingback shoe goes straight through a Styrofoam step. She limps along with her foot stuck in the Styrofoam block, and Eric and Ernie free her, removing both the block and the shoe. Shirley takes a few more limping steps with one foot bare before Eric slips his own size 10 hobnail boot on her. Shirley followed the comedy spot – after a quick change into a different sparkling evening gown, this time with cutaway sides and a dangerously low back – with a performance of 'Diamonds Are Forever.'

The show's producer John Ammonds recalled that Shirley 'got the full treatment from Eric. He was around when she was getting ready to record her solo spot on the show. She'd got her "Diamonds Are Forever" outfit on, you know, covered in all the sequins with the star filters on the camera to get all those sparkling effects, and Eric wandered over to her and said, "Christ! You look like a bloody Brillo pad!" And Shirley laughed. Anybody else and she would probably have hit them, but not Eric!'

In spring 1972 Shirley undertook a 12-date US tour that saw her receiving standing ovations and breaking box-office records at New York's Lincoln Center. When asked, Shirley stated that she now preferred to play larger venues whenever possible: 'I'm a little fed up with nightclubs because it's too long – you're in a place two or three weeks. It's better constantly moving – different houses, different audiences.'

*

On the home front, since their villa in Lugano was still being built, Sergio and Shirley bought another villa, in Sardinia, and made that their primary home for a while. They took holidays in the mountains in Cortina, and also at the beach, and Shirley said that she liked to 'play tennis, swim and frolic on the beach with the children.' Long afterwards Shirley recalled, 'I had so many happy times there. I helped design the villa in Sardinia. It was by the sea with a turret, so I had a round bedroom and a round staircase. I lived there for about 10 years until the kids grew up, then I got divorced. It was beautiful, with its own beach, its own pier, its own boat.'

On a visit back to Britain, Shirley found herself the subject of an episode of TV's *This Is Your Life* ('Don't do this to me,' was her immediate response to host Eamonn Andrews and his famous red book), while *TV Times* magazine named her 'Best Female Singer' of the year (she won the title again the following year). Just as well, since her albums that year *I, Capricorn* and *And I Love You So*, had both been fairly unremarkable.

Sharon Novak had turned 18 that year, and had returned to London to begin her own working life; after a brief period working in a haute-couture dress shop, she took up a career as a nursery nurse. Samantha and Mark were now away at Swiss boarding schools, and Shirley only saw them during school holidays. The rest of the time, she toured the world: Japan, Europe, Australia, the USA and elsewhere. Sometimes Sergio accompanied her, sometimes he was working on deals for her in an office on the other side of the world. Over the next few years their marriage appeared to be under a good deal of strain, and Shirley was said to be drinking more than she usually did.

Her 1973 album *Never Never Never* made the UK Top Ten (as did the single release of the title song, which also went to Number One in Australia). The title song was another one that Shirley had discovered, which was originally an Italian ballad called 'Grande, Grande, Grande'; it became her biggest US hit since 'Goldfinger', and her US fans now thronged to see her in concert. She undertook another US tour in the spring, which included two dates at New York's Carnegie Hall with Woody Herman and the Young Thundering Herd; these were recorded for an extremely good album, *Live At Carnegie Hall*, which was released the following year.

In 1974, Shirley was named 'Best Female Singer' by *Music Week*, and released the *Nobody Does It Like Me* album. She also played a week's cabaret in Paris that summer, making her debut at L'Espace, a fashionable venue created by the fashion designer Pierre Cardin. Cardin threw an elaborate opening night party for her at the famous Paris restaurant Maxim's. At a concert at the Royal Albert Hall that October, David Frost interrupted the show to present Shirley with no less than 10 gold discs for album sales.

In spring 1975, Shirley returned to Carnegie Hall to play five consecutive nights which sold out almost immediately, breaking the venue's house record in the process. Reviewing the show, New York's *Daily Post* called Shirley 'the world's greatest female entertainer.' That year she released another album, *Good, Bad But Beautiful*, and filmed a Christmas special for BBC TV.

The following year, 1976, saw Shirley celebrating her twentieth anniversary as a recording artist with a 22-date British tour and a new album, *Love, Life And Feelings*. On the other side of the Atlantic, she was named 'Best Female Entertainer' by the American Guild of Variety Artists. That autumn she starred in her own Saturday night BBC TV series, which featured sequences filmed in exotic locations around the world, as well as in the TV studio; her musical guests for the series included Neil Diamond, Dusty Springfield and Janis Ian. Commenting on the fact that Shirley was then nearing 40, *Radio Times* observed: 'Very few artists do so well for so long and she is very much the same Shirley Bassey throughout. A bit plumper now, perhaps, and a little more rounded in the face. And her dresses do not reveal as much as of yore.' It went on to add that Shirley's 'thirst for adulation' made her 'at times a truly disturbing artist.'

At some point around 1977, Shirley and Sergio's marriage finally hit the rocks for good. Mark Novak later recalled that his parents had stopped arguing; and since fighting had been part of the dynamic that had always made their marriage work, this was not a good sign: 'They seemed to live in a boxing ring, and when they stopped fighting, that was it, their marriage was over.' Accounts differ as to when Shirley and Sergio actually separated, but it was either 1978 or 1979. Muriel Burgess reports that Shirley announced her pending divorce at a press conference at London's Dorchester Hotel, where she told reporters: 'I won't make the same mistake again, because I shan't get married again.'

Shirley would later blame the collapse of her marriage on the fact that she had allowed Sergio to become her manager: 'My first husband was in the business, so it was more like a partnership. I didn't learn from my mistake, I did it again and, second time, it was even worse. We were talking about contracts in bed.' She also ruefully observed that, 'Moneywise, I've looked after all the men in my life.'

Sergio Novak, on the other hand, would later claim that the marriage finally ended because Shirley was having an affair with her Australian road manager Kenny Carter (which, according to Muriel Burgess, was confirmed by Shirley's then-secretary Hilary Levy). Regardless, the divorce would seem to have been a bitter one. 'She was overdosing on fame,' Sergio later claimed. 'Her stardom transferred to her private life. And Shirley has a bad temper.' Decades later, Shirley would dismissively refer to her second husband on stage as simply 'the Italian.'

t w e l v e

THE LOSS

After her divorce from Sergio Novak, Kenny McArthur became Shirley's new manager and agent. Kenny Carter remained her road manager for only a few more years before leaving (possibly because their romance had already come to an end).

In 1978 came the release of the *Shirley Bassey 25^(th) Anniversary* greatest hits collection, which made the UK Top Ten (as *The Shirley Bassey Singles Album* had done three years earlier). In all, between 1970 and 1979 Shirley had 18 hit albums in the UK charts. That year Shirley also won a special Brit Award, for the 'Best British female solo artist during the past 25 years.'

Otherwise, the year's major event took place one evening in December. Shirley and a party of friends had gone out for dinner at a restaurant in Fulham, and then carried on their celebrations at a house in Eaton Square. After the neighbours had repeatedly complained about the noise, the police arrived on the scene to investigate. Inside the house they found a drunken Shirley among the guests, singing 'Quando, Quando' at the top of her voice. She was told to keep quiet, but refused to do so, and kept on singing – and at some point soon after that, she was arrested. As she was led outside ('distraught and agitated,' according to Muriel Burgess) she reportedly pushed one of the policemen in the back. When arrested, Shirley had told police that her name was 'Shirley Carter', but they weren't fooled for a moment; she was taken to Gerard Road police station and charged – under her real name – with being drunk and disorderly. On 21 December Shirley appeared before Horseferry Road Magistrates Court. Her defence counsel referred to Shirley as 'a lady of unblemished character', and she personally apologized for causing a disturbance on the evening in question. The magistrate bound her over for three months, but stated that he was sure she would not re-offend. It was, perhaps, a sign that Shirley's drinking was starting to become a serious problem.

In 1979, Shirley recorded her third and final theme song for a James Bond film, 'Moonraker'. John Barry had originally recorded a version of this song with Johnny Mathis, but afterwards felt that his vocals lacked the necessary oomph; a chance meeting between Barry and Shirley in the lobby of the Beverley Hills Hotel led to her being drafted in to help out, and within days she was recording the song in a studio in Los Angeles. Unfortunately, at this point the 007 franchise was at a very low ebb, since the Roger Moore years had seen Bond reduced to one-dimensional status as a character, and all of the later Moore films were more light comedy in tone than action-adventure. And despite the presence of Burt Bacharach's collaborator Hal David as lyricist, Barry's theme song was also a pale imitation of his earlier triumphs – something that Shirley herself was doubtless aware of, although when asked about the song at the time she simply said, 'I think it's great to be the only singer to have sung three Bond songs. It's a wonderful honour.' Shirley also recorded two albums that year, *The Magic Is You* and *What I Did For Love*, and filmed a second season of her BBC TV show. September saw her appearing for a run at New York's Minskoff Theatre, billed as *Shirley Bassey on Broadway*. In November she played at the Royal Performance at Wembley Conference Centre, in front of Prince Charles.

It was also in 1979, or possibly in 1980, that Shirley became a grandmother for the first time, when Sharon gave birth to a son named Luke. Rumours that Shirley was contemplating retirement had been appearing in magazine articles for some time; to silence them, in 1981 she announced her own plans to 'semi-retire'. She stated her intention to cut down on touring, and to be even more selective in her choice of venues and dates. In reality, there seemed to be very little easing up at all – during one year in the 1980s, Shirley played concerts in Australia, Austria, Canada, England, France, Germany, Holland, Hong Kong, Ireland, Japan, Poland, Scotland, Sri Lanka, Turkey, the United Arab Emirates, the USA and Wales. On top of this, she played charity benefits, recorded records and made TV appearances. So much for slowing down! However, she had bought herself a new villa in Marbella, in Southern Spain, and was known to take lengthy holidays there.

That year, 1981, Shirley's mother died suddenly in her sleep, three days after her eightieth birthday. Eliza Mendi had been suffering from low blood pressure, and probably died from some heart-related illness. Although Shirley had seen her mother regularly, she usually only met the rest of her family when she was playing concerts in Cardiff, after which they would all join her backstage to catch up on family gossip. Shirley's sister Eileen had described such a meeting in the 1960s: 'Shirley gets a bit confused at times when the whole family with all our children pile into her dressing room after the show. But they don't stay long, and then we sisters and Henry, our brother, get an hour with her. And the champagne flows. There's lots of gossip and cross-questioning and hugs and kisses. She tells us about her trips abroad and her cabaret shows.'

On the day of Eliza's funeral in Cardiff this lack of closeness would have unfortunate consequences. Shirley was 'in the most terrible state. I felt rootless, as if my life had been torn apart. She had never doubted me, and she has always been there for me.' She wept freely, and – perhaps as a result of a few drinks at the family gathering after Eliza's funeral – an argument broke out there between Shirley and some of her sisters, supposedly over Eliza's treatment of their father, with the result that Shirley left the party abruptly. Since neither side apologized for what had been said at the party, the argument created a family rift which supposedly lasted for some years, although it is believed to have been mended some time ago. However, it remains noticeable that in recent years Dame Shirley has only returned to Cardiff to play concerts there. The rift was probably fuelled further when Shirley's sister Marina sold her story to the papers, claiming that Shirley had effectively sidelined her family. 'My success became a barrier with my family,' Shirley said much later. 'They couldn't relate to me and I couldn't relate to them. But then, I never could. I was just in the way.'

*

In 1982, Shirley courted controversy when she played a concert in Sun City, South Africa's expensive leisure resort in Bophuthatswana. Although race had never really been an issue for Shirley personally, she was obviously well aware of the evils of South Africa's apartheid policy, and she subsequently stated that she had mistakenly believed that the Sun City resort – which was not racially segregated – was not actually a part of South Africa: 'I would never perform in Johannesburg, Durban or Cape Town. But I went to Sun City because it was a fantastic project, and they didn't stop blacks from going there.'

But for Shirley's critics, playing Sun City meant that she had supported the regime in South Africa (if only passively), as a result of which she attracted a great deal of negative publicity. In the UK anti-apartheid demonstrators picketed some her concerts, and she was placed on a United Nations blacklist. 'If you are an entertainer, you entertain,' Shirley responded. 'I don't like politicians telling us what to do.' To be fair, she was by no means alone in making the mistake of playing at the resort, as numerous other British and American acts had done so (a roster that includes Frank Sinatra, Elton John, Cher, Liza Minnelli, Rod Stewart and Queen). Years on from the collapse of apartheid this may all seem of little importance, yet it's arguable that it was only world pressure – in the form of sanctions and boycotts – that helped bring about the much-needed political change in South Africa. Shirley did what she could to undo the damage to her reputation at the time by publicly pledging that she would never perform in South Africa or any other country where segregation of any kind was practised. That year, Shirley also released the album *All By Myself*.

She had a brief stint in hospital in 1983, as she was suffering from digestive problems. This led her to give up various foods, including red meat, since she had trouble digesting it. She hasn't eaten it since. In 1984 Shirley recorded an album of her most famous songs with the London Symphony Orchestra (conducted by Carl Davis), *I Am What I Am*. The title track – the ultimate statement of gay pride from the musical *La Cage Aux Folles* – was also released as a single. That year Shirley's secretary Hilary Levy left her employ, after working for her for six years, but would eventually return.

In May 1985, Shirley sang at a gala charity concert at St David's Hall in Cardiff, in aid of the International Youth Year for Wales. But the rest of the year would be dominated by a much darker event: the unexpected death of her younger daughter Samantha.

*

Samantha had left her Swiss boarding school (where she was seemingly a bit of a rebel) at the age of 18. She then signed on for a course at Bristol Technical College, but dropped out after only six months; after this, she continued to live in Bristol, where she led a fairly aimless existence for the following year and a half, doing very little and spending much of her time in various pubs with her friends.

Then, one day in August 1985, Shirley flew from Lugano to Heathrow Airport, expecting to rendezvous there with her musical director and dresser before flying on with them to the Far East to commence a concert tour. According to Muriel Burgess, much to Shirley's surprise she was met at Heathrow by Sharon, who broke the news to her that Samantha's dead body had been discovered in the river Avon (it had been spotted by tourists on a pleasure boat). She had been missing for over a week.

The next day Shirley's manager Tony MacArthur issued a press statement that read, 'Miss Bassey is staying with friends in London. It is devastating news but she is handling the situation very well.' The first press reports indicated that Samantha must have either fallen or thrown herself off of the Clifton Suspension Bridge – which has long been a popular location for suicidal jumpers – since her fully clothed body had been discovered in the river a quarter of a mile downstream from the bridge. This theory has been repeated down the years as unchallenged fact, despite being simply a case of lazy journalism; the fact is that there is no evidence whatsoever that Samantha was ever on the bridge at all, and her body bore no injuries consistent with a fall. The truth would appear to be that Samantha died from a heart attack, almost certainly brought on by the shock of suddenly plunging into freezing river water.

Shirley has always refused to believe that Samantha's death was suicide, and later stated, 'She had my resolve. She was strong like me.' On another occasion she dismissed the theory with the words, 'There's no proof of it whatsoever.' The coroner agreed with her: Samantha's death was almost certainly a tragic accident. She had gone drinking with friends, and was last seen walking towards the river bank. There was nothing in her manner to suggest that she was unhappy or disturbed, and the coroner concluded that, 'It is possible that she may have walked by the river and perhaps tripped. If Samantha was slightly fuddled with drink, she may have slipped down the river bank. Samantha died from the shock of hitting the water. She was an able swimmer but the shock of hitting the cold water killed her.'

Samantha's funeral took place on 12 September 1985 in Westbury, near Bristol. The grief-stricken Shirley was physically supported by her friend Soraya Khashoggi, and her daughter Sharon. Among the floral tributes was a wreath from Dionne Warwick, and another from Samantha's favourite band, the Grateful Dead; one of Samantha's favourite songs, Jimi Hendrix's 'Foxy Lady' was played during the brief service.

Some of the press coverage of Samantha's death was sympathetic, but many of the tabloids also implied that Shirley had been a neglectful mother, and thus somehow responsible for the tragedy. But Shirley was already 'riddled with guilt', and there was no accusation that could be levelled at her that she hadn't already thought of herself. 'I tortured myself,' she later disclosed. 'Samantha's death had been my fault. If I'd been a better mother . . . So many thoughts run through your head. Your children are supposed to bury you, not the other way around.' Shirley blamed herself for the fact that, time after time, she had left her children with a nanny while she had gone away on tour. She had also bought them extravagant presents as a way of compensating for her lengthy absences, and now wondered if she had spoiled them – and also wondered if she had been strict enough, or physically demonstrative enough: 'I never disciplined my children and I suppose that made me a bad mother. I was never disciplined by my mother. I never knew what discipline was. My mother never told me off or spanked me. As I grew up I began to fear that the men in my life would try and tame me. If you tried to discipline me now you would just get abuse. It's too late. Come to think of it, there was no contact of any kind in my family. There was not a lot of love. We were not tactile.' That lack of physical closeness had also been carried on in Shirley's relationship with her own children: 'I probably cuddled them more, but not much more. If you've had that as a child, you will have it as a grown-up. I'm not demonstrative. I have to pretend on stage. Pretend to be the tactile person I would like to be.' But behind all the self-recrimination was simple, overwhelming sadness, and a sense of deep loss: 'She talked like me. I saw me in her. I thought she'd be an actress and go on the stage . . . but now we'll never know what she was capable of.'

Anyone who has lost a loved one in tragic and/or mysterious circumstances knows how much harder it is to endure than an ordinary death; those who have not experienced it simply cannot imagine it. What has seemed unnecessarily cruel to Shirley over the years has been the way that every time the press do a new story about her, Samantha's death is invariably mentioned as well, and is almost always described as a suicide. 'Every time someone writes that it's like a stab of pain to my heart,' Shirley has said. 'Samantha would never have done that. She enjoyed having a go at me too much. She had my resolve and was strong like me.' Dredging up old 'facts' from their files is part of the way the mainstream press operates, but to Shirley it remains unforgivable. 'They're evil,' she said on one occasion. 'Not all of them, but . . .'

Shirley's grief would be long-lasting (as witness the fact that her 2007 album *Get The Party Started* is dedicated to Samantha), and would affect her on many levels. It was, at least, something to which Shirley's fans were deeply sensitive. When Shirley walked on stage at New York's Carnegie Hall two weeks after Samantha's death wearing a black gown (albeit one decorated with a stylized orchid made of Swarovski crystals), the audience gave her a five-minute-long standing ovation before she'd even sung a note, in sympathy with her pain. 'Their response was incredible, so uplifting,' Shirley said afterwards. 'It was a real effort to keep control. I just kept telling myself that if I cried my eyelashes would fall off and my mascara would run all over my face. But when the orchestra started to play 'When You're Smiling' it just all came together. They got me through, but I hardly knew what I was doing. One part of me was quite numb. All my grief was locked away and this wonderful audience helped and comforted me with their understanding and loving support for what I was going through.' After Carnegie Hall, Shirley carried on with the rest of her American tour, and then moved on to play more concerts in Europe. She was keeping herself busy, constantly on the move as if this might somehow hold the grief at bay indefinitely – but as Shirley's manager Tony MacArthur acutely observed at the time: 'She is handling it all very well, she is going on with her tour. But one day the finality of it all will really hit her.'

And it did. It happened in Australia – the country where Samantha might very well have been conceived – in January 1986. Shirley was playing a concert at the Sydney Centre when, for the first time since the early days of her career, she lost her voice. 'I walked out in front of 10,000 people in Sydney, opened my mouth to sing 'Goldfinger' and nothing came out,' she later said. 'I tried again and nothing. It was like a nightmare. I wanted the stage to open up.'

thirteen

THE SURVIVOR

'The amazing thing was that nobody booed,' Shirley later said of the Sydney concert. She feared that – having lost her voice once – it could happen again, but also realized that the problem was almost certainly an emotional one, rather than simply something physical. But even though, she was aware that 'guilt is a terrible thing to carry around. It makes you ill', she had no means of expressing her feelings, as she later explained: 'I was grieving. The trouble was, I had nobody to talk to about my daughter's death. I couldn't even talk to my other daughter about it. I was guilt-ridden. By not being able to talk to anyone I hadn't been able to come to terms with it. The shock had been too much. Even when I got past that stage and went back to work, I thought, "Don't talk to anyone about it because they really don't want to listen." Which was true. People didn't want to know. I would start talking about it and they would always interrupt with something that happened to them, as a way of comforting me, I suppose. But no one had an equivalent story to mine. My only option was to go to a therapist who I could pay just to listen. But I didn't. I didn't want to get hooked on that. I know too many people who get hooked on therapy.'

But therapy was what she needed. Instead, Shirley went home to Switzerland and became a virtual recluse, spending her days comfort-eating chocolate and cheese. 'I'd wake in the night and go to the fridge to get a bar of chocolate and a big lump of cheese – and I mean really big. It got to the stage where I was having to wear a maternity dress.' After nearly a year of this behaviour, she realized that 'sitting around feeling sorry for myself wasn't going to help me, and it wouldn't bring back Samantha.' She then checked herself in to a health clinic in Los Angeles to get professional help, and stayed there for 10 days. While in the clinic she began an exercise regime to lose weight: 'It worked wonders, it was like a form of brainwashing. They re-educated me to be so careful about what I eat.' It seems likely that it was also during this period that Shirley began to cut back drastically on her drinking, which had got out of hand during the later years of her marriage to Sergio. Her son Mark later commented that, 'It took Shirley a long time to give up heavy drinking. But she did.'

Shirley's next move was to sell the Villa Capricorn, after which she moved temporarily into a hotel in Lausanne for a short while before finally leaving Switzerland for good: 'My instinct had been to hide behind my mountain. But after a while the mountain got closer. The place was getting smaller. Peter Finch told me when he was leaving Switzerland that every morning the mountains were getting that much closer. It was chilling. It came true for me. One morning they had come closer.'

Shirley needed to get back to work, but she was still concerned that her voice might fail her. She had continued to have problems with it, and even when she didn't she feared that they might return at any moment; in her worst moments, she feared her talent had left her for good and 'began to think there was no way out of the problem.' Finally, she consulted a throat specialist in London, who recommended that she should seek advice and help from a former opera singer named Helena Shenel, who was now practising as a voice coach.

Helena taught Shirley some operatic vocal exercises that enabled her to gain complete control of her voice. 'After a year, my vocal chords had been strengthened and the physical problem was over,' Shirley later said; she also commented that, 'Going to Helena Shenel was the best thing I have ever done and her advice about vocal exercises was the best advice I have ever been given.' Shirley had learned how to avoid overreaching herself, and in the process her vocal range had even increased by an octave, and she could now sing perfectly even while suffering from a heavy cold.

With her confidence restored, she could now begin performing again, and her vocal problems were finally over. Years later, she commented that, 'Since I've been doing the exercises my voice has never let me down.' Despite the voice problems, Shirley still managed to do some recording during 1986, and had a minor hit with a song titled 'There's No Place Like London', which was written by Linsey De Paul and Gerard Kenny.

She still needed to feel better about herself as a mother. But Samantha was dead, and her son Mark had refused to go to university and had become somewhat of a layabout; he was living in Marbella, and got by on an allowance from Shirley and by doing various casual jobs. He wouldn't listen to his mother's advice, and over time they drifted further and further apart. Inevitably, with nowhere else to invest her maternal feelings, Shirley grew much closer to Sharon and her son, though she also confessed that 'I make a much better grandmother than I ever did a mother.'

*

Shirley's career had by now settled into a well-established pattern of touring and recording; she had a loyal fan following and knew how to please them, and no one expected that scenario to change too radically. Then, in March 1987, Shirley recorded the first of what would become a series of collaborations with much younger pop artists. There was a vogue for this kind of collaboration during the 1980s, with the Smiths championing Sandie Shaw, Heaven 17 accompanying Tina Turner and the Pet Shop Boys working with both Dusty Springfield and Liza Minnelli.

Shirley's first one was with the Swiss electro-pop duo Yello (otherwise known as Dieter Meier and Boris Blank). The group had become friendly with the Scottish singer Billy MacKenzie of the Associates during 1986, and he had supplied backing vocals to several tracks on the group's 1987 album *One Second*. MacKenzie also co-wrote one song with Boris Blank, 'The Rhythm Divine', which all concerned felt deserved something special in terms of its lead vocal. Although a version of the song with vocals by Billy MacKenzie surfaced in a compilation after his death (sadly, MacKenzie died in 1997, having committed suicide at the age of 39), according to Dieter Meier these were simply 'guide vocals' intended to sell the song to the person they really wanted to sing it, and there was never any doubt as to who that was going to be.

'Shirley was our first and only choice as a vocalist,' Meier confirmed to me in 2007. 'A mutual friend, Hubertus von Hohenlohe, had played Shirley some of our music and got her interested in recording a track with us. Once we presented the track to Shirley – with Billy's guide vocals in place – everything went very smooth and quick. She flew in from Spain and recorded the vocals within two to three hours at our studio in Zurich. Shirley was very professional and very easy to work with, and we were all very pleased with the result.' At the time he stated that 'Shirley Bassey has one of the greatest voices I have ever heard, and a strength as a performer that's rare.'

The song itself was an atmospheric disco ballad that conjured up romantic images of trans-European train travel, name-checking both Warsaw and Rome. Billy MacKenzie provided no fewer than 90 layers of multi-tracked backing vocals for the song, and his family were apparently more impressed by this record than by anything else he'd ever done: 'Working with her made everything valid with my mum and aunties. It's smoothed out those family wrinkles.' Though the tune wasn't Yello's strongest work (or Shirley's), the record still got very good reviews and a lot of airplay, and undoubtedly brought Shirley to the attention of a younger audience. However, she herself seems to have been somewhat unhappy with the collaboration at the time; when she played at the Royal Albert Hall with a full orchestra a few months later, she introduced 'The Rhythm Divine' with the words: 'This is how the song *should* have sounded.'

In November, Shirley appeared in the Royal Variety Performance at the Palladium. That month she also attended the wedding of her daughter Sharon to Steve Barton, a builder from Henley-on-Thames. Sharon had obviously chosen the day especially, since it was Samantha's birthday. Outside the church, 50 of Shirley's loyal fans waited for a glimpse of her.

*

In 1988, Shirley took on another experimental project by recording *La Mujer*, an album canta en español – or to put it another way, sung entirely in Spanish; it was released the following year. The fact that Shirley didn't actually speak Spanish didn't deter her in the least from taking on the project. She simply signed up for 20 hours of Spanish lessons, which at least meant that her pronunciation was correct without her having to rely on someone writing down phonetic renditions of the lyrics.

After that, life returned to the old routine for a number of years. In 1989 Hilary Levy returned as Shirley's PA and secretary; in December 1990 Shirley appeared at a gala concert at the London Palladium in aid of the Prince's Trust, in front of the Prince and Princess of Wales.

In 1991 Shirley's album *Keep The Music Playing* included a cover version of Foreigner's 'I Want To Know What Love Is' (her most contemporary choice of material for some years). 'Nobody expected me to do that,' Shirley commented later. In May that year Shirley became a grandmother again, when her son Mark and his wife had a baby daughter, Tatjana. Sadly, their marriage didn't last for very long.

On stage at the Albert Hall in October, Shirley was ambushed by Michael Aspel, and consequently made her second appearance as the subject of the *This Is Your Life* TV show. Late in 1992 Shirley was at the Albert Hall again, this time for the Chelsea Arts Club Ball. Her son Mark was in the audience, at the front of the stage; he held up his 18-month-old daughter for Shirley to hold, and the proud grandmother held little Tatjana up for the audience to see.

At the very end of the year, it was announced that Shirley had been awarded the CBE in the New Year's Honours List, in recognition of all the time and money she had dedicated to numerous charities, including the Prince's Trust.

Accompanying Shirley to Buckingham Palace in January 1993 for the investiture ceremony by HM Queen Elizabeth II were her daughter Sharon and her close friends Beaudoin and Yves Mills. Afterwards, Shirley said that the award meant that 'all I have done has been recognized, not only by Her Majesty, but by the country where I was born.'

Later that year she released the album *Shirley Bassey Sings the Songs of Andrew Lloyd Webber*, its 13 tracks a representative selection drawn from all of the composer's musicals. That September Shirley performed at the opening concert of Cardiff's new International Arena, and was also made an Honorary Fellow of the Royal Welsh College of Music and Drama (she would later become a patron of the college).

*

In 1993, South Africa's apartheid regime had finally come to an end, and consequently Shirley and other Western performers were now able to tour in the country once again. After a post-concert party in Cape Town one night that December, Shirley had an argument with her secretary Hilary Levy which got out of hand. For many years Hilary had accepted the fact that working for Shirley was a 24/7 job; for example, if Shirley had insomnia, Hilary was expected to stay up and keep her company. It went with the job, and Hilary understood that – but on this particular occasion she felt that Shirley was making demands that were totally unreasonable. When the party ended it was already very early in the morning, and Shirley told Hilary that she wanted her to do some Christmas shopping for her before bringing her breakfast in bed at noon. As this would mean that Hilary got hardly any sleep, she objected. Hilary would later claim that this sparked a full-blown argument in which Shirley had fired her from her job on the spot, and had also hit her and called her a 'Jewish bitch.' She subsequently sued Shirley for lost earnings as a result of this. Shirley's response was to deny that she had fired her secretary, hit her or insulted her – although she did admit that she had pushed Hilary and called her a 'spoilt Jewish princess.' Beaudoin Mills, who had been at the party and witnessed part of the argument, tried to persuade Hilary not to walk out on her job immediately, but without success; he would eventually corroborate Shirley's version of the events in court – but it would take another four years before the case was heard.

*

In 1994 Shirley celebrated her fortieth anniversary in show business. During her UK tour she switched on the Blackpool illuminations, and was the subject of a Variety Club tribute luncheon at the Savoy. Once again she played at the Royal Variety Performance, which took place this time at the Dominion Theatre, where she received a lengthy standing ovation from the audience. That year also saw the release of a five-CD retrospective boxed set, *The EMI/UA Years*.

In July 1995 Shirley headlined a concert at Cardiff Castle. She also played a concert by the pyramids in Cairo that year, being one of the few artists ever to do so (the others being Frank Sinatra and the Grateful Dead). She won an award from the Variety Club of Great Britain, who named her 'Show Business Personality of the Year', and released the *Shirley Bassey Sings the Movies* album (which, as its title implies, featured a selection of well-known movie themes). In September of that year she recorded the TV show *An Audience with Shirley Bassey* for LWT, which was broadcast the following year. Her gowns for the show seemed to consist of carefully positioned lace or sequins and very little else. She then undertook her biggest UK tour to date – which included another Royal Gala performance.

In 1996 Shirley had a minor hit with 'Disco La Passione', from Chris Rea's movie *La Passione*. The film was Rea's semi-autobiographical fantasy of a young boy from an Italian immigrant family who is far more interested in becoming a Grand Prix racing driver than in taking over the family ice-cream business. Shirley appeared in the film (as herself), singing a rather bizarre duet with Rea, as well as a disco version of the film's theme tune. Sadly, the song itself is unremarkable, though once again it meant that Shirley's voice could be heard in clubs, and by a much younger audience than the one she usually attracted.

*

The following year, 1997, saw yet another collaboration, but this time a far more successful one, when Shirley was asked to record a song with the British electronic producers Will White and Alex Gifford, otherwise known as the Propellerheads. The band was immensely hip and would become even more so, at least partly due to their music appearing on the soundtrack of the film *The Matrix*. Released the following year, the band's album *Decksanddrumsandrockandroll* included their collaboration with Shirley, 'History Repeating', a fusion of jazz and Big Beat, which went to number one on the British Dance Music charts (appropriately, the album also contained the band's version of a Bond movie theme, 'On Her Majesty's Secret Service'). Alex Gifford later commented that he and White had 'just always wanted to do a song in the old style, like a classic song. We were thinking who could possibly be best to sing it, and we both immediately thought of Shirley Bassey. We did a demo of it and sent it to her management. A little while later we heard she was up for doing it.'

At first Shirley had her doubts about the song, feeling that it was more suited to someone like Tina Turner; then she discovered that Alex Gifford had written it with her in mind, and so felt that it would be churlish to turn it down. 'He said he was asleep, and he thought about me, and these words came out,' she told the *Miami New Times*. 'And I asked, "What's a 35-year-old man doing thinking about a grandmother?" I couldn't imagine!' When Alex told Shirley that he was actually only 33 years old she replied, 'My God! I have a son your age.'

Feeling that they couldn't really expect Shirley to record in 'our hovel in Bath', the Propellerheads booked time at a studio in London, 'got the champagne and roses in and wore our best shirts' in readiness for Shirley's arrival. They were still unprepared for the reality: 'Of course, she was absolutely terrifying when she swanned in. The shades never came off, but she was really very warm. The total star.'

The group asked Shirley to sing her vocal lower and lower, until she reached a point where she was sounding positively gravel-voiced. When she first heard the results, Shirley thought she 'sounded like Louis Armstrong.' Gifford later admitted that while Shirley was recording her vocal, the hairs stood up all over his body, an experience he described as 'chilling.' As for Shirley, she decided to trust the group's judgement: 'I still don't believe that it's my voice. It's incredible, I mean, I've never sung like that before. It's like a new me.'

The cover notes of the *Decksanddrumsandrockandroll* album read: 'We would like to extend our maximum respect to Shirley Bassey for honouring us with her performance. We are still in shock . . .' The song was also subsequently included on the soundtrack of the hit comedy movie *There's Something About Mary* (one of the top-grossing films of 1998), as well as becoming the theme tune for Channel 4's *So Graham Norton* show. It's a curiously old-fashioned dance number, its lyrics taking a cynical assessment of the cyclical nature of politics and fashion, and the fickleness of the latter.

Shirley and the Propellerheads also shot a video for the song, with director Pedro Romani, which required her to lip-synch with her recorded vocal. 'I'm hopeless at miming,' Shirley protested before they began. 'I'm a live entertainer.' During the filming Shirley had to stand for three hours on a revolving dais, wearing a dress that was so heavy that she couldn't actually lift it up in emergencies ('I couldn't even go for a pee'); she found herself almost unable to move and 'in agony the next morning.' The second day she had to endure two more hours of make-up for close-up re-shoots because 'they'd made the cheeks too puffy and I looked like a chipmunk.' Publicity shots for the single show Shirley in a zebra-striped dress, linking arms with White and Gifford; she looked like a cross between the ultimate glamorous granny and a cat who'd got the cream.

The record undoubtedly altered Shirley's demographic, as she later explained: 'Now I've got young kids – I mean, really, even six- and seven-year-olds – coming up to me on the street and saying, "I love your new record. I'm a big fan!".' She also told reporters that she was now performing 'History Repeating' live: 'I have to! Everybody's waiting for it. They don't think I'm going to do it, but when I do, they howl!' In concert, Shirley would make the audience clap along to the rhythm of the song in time with her.

*

That year Shirley attended Elton John's fiftieth birthday party, and also celebrated her own sixtieth birthday. To mark the occasion, she played two huge open-air concerts, at Castle Howard and Althorp Park. The resulting live recording *The Birthday Concert* was nominated for a Grammy in the Best Traditional Female Vocal Performance category (although a banner on the cover claims the concert was recorded at Althorp Park, smaller print in the sleeve notes reveals that it was recorded at both venues). Her tour that autumn took her to Antwerp, diamond capital of the world; understandably, Shirley took advantage of this fact by having a clause inserted in her contract that, in addition to her fee, she would be given a pair of diamond earrings by the promoters. This tour was also filmed for a TV documentary, *Shirley Bassey – This Is My Life*, which can be found on the live *Divas Are Forever* DVD.

*

In January 1998, the court case between Shirley Bassey and Hilary Levy was finally heard at Brentford County Court, before Judge Marcus Edwards. Hilary was suing Shirley for breach of contract and over £7,000 in lost earnings. Shirley – who denied all the charges – broke down in tears while giving evidence. 'I have fought this case regardless of cost in order to defend my name and reputation and as a point of principle,' she said. Although Beaudoin Mills had also given evidence, the case was largely a matter of one woman's word against another's; summing up, the judge called Hilary 'an unpersuasive witness', but referred to Shirley as being both 'persuasive' and 'a straightforward person.' The court awarded her costs.

Outside the court, Shirley emerged to cheers from a crowd of waiting fans, and told waiting reporters that she thought Hilary had been 'vindictive. She had a good job and she walked out on me. She accused me of firing her, which was untrue, and of being anti-Semitic, which was untrue, and of hitting her, which was also untrue. The judge believed me. I am very distressed but I don't hate her. She was just saying what she thought she could get away with. But the truth will out, as it always does.' It was the charge of anti-Semitism that had really stung Shirley, and made her determined to defend her reputation in court at all costs. 'I have been in show business, which is full of Jewish people, for 45 years,' she stated. 'I have a Jewish manager, Jewish friends, Jewish boyfriends. I also have a daughter who is half-Jewish.' Shirley accepted a bouquet of roses from a fan, and then tossed each one of them into the throng, before departing in a black Mercedes.

*

That year Shirley's UK tour saw her playing to a total audience of over 120,000. This included 10 shows at London's Royal Festival Hall (breaking a house record she herself had set some years earlier), and two concerts at the Cardiff International Arena in May. She was back in Wales several times during 1999, having recorded 'World In Union' with the opera singer Bryn Terfel as the official theme song of the Rugby World Cup. On the first of November, Shirley and Bryn performed the song with a Welsh choir at the opening ceremony at the Millennium Stadium in Cardiff – and five days later they appeared again, with Michael Ball, at the contest's closing ceremony, this time singing 'We'll Keep a Welcome in the Hillsides.' On both occasions Shirley wore a kaftan dress designed by Sara Perceval which featured the Welsh 'dragon' flag. She had always felt that she had to give better than her best in Cardiff, and this was the ultimate Cardiff gig. 'That was such an emotional event for me,' she later admitted. 'An unforgettable moment in my career.'

At the end of the year, the New Year's Honours List was announced, and contained the news that Shirley Bassey had just been made a Dame Commander of the British Empire.

fourteen

THE DAME

Shirley Bassey had to keep the news of her damehood a secret for seven weeks, from early November 1999 until the New Year's Honours List was officially announced at the end of the year. 'I nearly had a nervous breakdown,' she later confessed. 'I was afraid to go out in case I told someone.' In May 2000 the newly appointed Dame sang 'Diamonds Are Forever' at a Cinema Against AIDS event which was part of the Cannes Film Festival, to raise money for the American AIDS charity amfAR.

The investiture ceremony for Shirley's DBE took place at Buckingham Palace in July. Dame Shirley was accompanied on the day by Beaudoin Mills, her daughter Sharon and her grandson Luke. She later said that she'd been almost moved to tears when the Queen congratulated her on her lengthy career. After the ceremony, she left almost immediately for Las Vegas, where she was due to play in cabaret at the MGM Grand Hotel.

*

That October, Dame Shirley was one of 80 guests selected by Sir Cliff Richard to accompany him on a week-long cruise around the

Mediterranean on board the ship *Seabourn Goddess I* in order to celebrate his sixtieth birthday. Dame Shirley and Sir Cliff had first met backstage at the *Six-Five Special* TV show in 1957, when she was 20 and he was just 17.

The year 2000 also saw the release of *The Remix Album: Diamonds Are Forever*, in which a collection of 10 top dance bands and DJs produced their own radically updated versions of Bassey classics. It was released on EMI, who owned the original recordings. As the album's A&R co-ordinator Nick Robinson told me, the project came about as a result of the success of Dame Shirley's earlier collaboration with the Propellerheads: 'The Propellerheads thing was a definite influence, as Shirley had enjoyed working with them and it was a successful record. The A&R guys at EMI and myself had considered various ideas for a new Shirley album and it just seemed to make sense at that time to go for a dance crossover hybrid – to follow up that previous success. And when EMI approached Shirley with the idea, she was excited about it and took little persuading.'

Robinson's next step was to draw up a list of possible artists to approach. 'I knew there were a lot of contemporary artists and producers in the dance world that loved her music, and many top DJs were known to drop her versions of "Spinning Wheel" and "Light My Fire" into their sets. So I wanted to get a mix of established names and newer, up-and-coming talents. I also didn't want to have three or four versions of the same songs and tried to get a broad range. I started by asking key people like Groove Armada, Masters At Work (Kenny Dope) and Nightmares On Wax whether they were fans of Shirley and if they'd be interested in doing a remix. It was their responses that basically helped me decide which ones to go for. Obviously, I was more interested in the ones that were big fans and seemed desperate to get involved. That's exactly what happened with those first three acts, and to be honest I don't think anyone flat out turned it down. Everyone seemed to be a fan, and if it didn't work out it was really a timing issue with people being already booked up or whatever. Also, it was great that the same songs didn't come up too often. I think Nightmares On Wax, Groove Armada and Moloko (DJ Skymoo) didn't go for obvious songs and yet came up with very inspired remixes. They also helped give the whole album a balance between the bigger, funkier tunes and the more downtempo, chilled-out numbers and I think that's why the album works as a whole and is not a weak mish-mash of tracks.'

Shirley gave the project her initial blessing, and then trusted Robinson's judgement when it came to selecting the artists, without insisting on hearing examples of their work herself. 'Obviously she wanted to hear the finished results and approve them, which of course I expected. So really her involvement was at the very start and at the end. But there was one instance where I called on her. I had approached the French production team Superfunk and they had shown an interest in doing a remix so I sent them the parts for one of the songs. They did a version of "Moonraker", but to my total surprise also sent me back a completely new instrumental that they had written. They attached a note that simply said, "Can Shirley add some vocals?" Of course, there were no lyrics so I was a little flummoxed! But we liked the tune, and I liked the idea of having one completely new tune on the album.' Robinson wrote some lyrics, and made plans to get Shirley into the studio, but scheduling problems meant that it never happened. 'So that great number-one-hit-to-be never quite made it!'

The final list of those taking part in the project was Groove Armada, the Propellerheads, awayTeam, Kenny Dope, Nightmares On Wax, Mantronix, DJ Spinna, Wild Oscar, Twelftree and DJ Skymoo (aka Moloko). The finished album was approved by Dame Shirley, as Robinson confirms: 'Shirley loved all the versions and only had one slight criticism on the awayTeam version of "Where Do I Begin." On hearing the track, she spotted that they had changed the key of one of her notes, by the miracle of modern samplers. I wouldn't have noticed it, but of course she did as she is so familiar with the original vocal. The awayTeam said they had to change the note as it did not fit the rhythm that they had sped up slightly. Anyway, they managed to adjust it so that everyone was happy in the end.'

Once released, the remix album 'got great reactions generally. Most of the reviews were favourable and commented that Shirley's vocal stylings suited the dance genre. "Light My Fire" and "Where Do I Begin" especially continue to appear on many of those Hotel/Bar compilations around the world. I also read an article in Q magazine a little while ago in which TV personality Lawrence Llewelyn Bowen commented that it was one of his favourite ever albums.' As might have been expected, the album was a very mixed bag indeed, and in many cases it must be said that the remixes were decidedly inferior to the original records. That said, awayTeam's treatment of 'Where Do I Begin' really works (and was released as a single), as does Groove Armada's version of 'Never Never Never';

but easily the best track on the album is the comparatively obscure 'Easy Thing To Do', transformed by Nightmares On Wax from a simple, quiet ballad into a masterpiece of restrained funk. Regardless, Robinson was more than pleased with the overall results: 'I had a fantastic time making that album and everyone involved was a joy to work with. I think all of us were honoured to be playing a part in the project. Overall, I'm just proud of the fact that the whole concept worked and that Dame Shirley once again proved that her voice transcends all genres. She's a dance diva too!'

The last album sold well right across Europe, as did the 'Where Do I Begin' single; to promote the latter, a computer-animated video was commissioned, with a robotic 3D 'Shirley' performing the song in the style of a 1930s musical. 'It's weird,' Dame Shirley commented of the record's success. 'Just when I'm thinking of taking it easy, something magical happens and off we go again.' Damehood wasn't the only honour she was given in 2000, either; she was also presented with UNESCO's Artist for Peace award.

*

After the excitements of the previous year, 2001 seemed to be comparatively quiet for Dame Shirley, the highlight being her performance at the Royal Albert Hall in May at an event to celebrate Prince Philip's eightieth birthday. In February 2002, Dame Shirley attended the wedding of Joan Collins (her fifth, to Percy Gibson), dressed all in red and sporting a red beret, 'just like Little Red Riding Hood.' At the reception at Claridge's Hotel Dame Shirley sang Perry Como's 'And I Love You So' for the bride and groom. That summer she appeared as one of the guest artists at

Party at the Palace, part of the celebrations for HM Queen Elizabeth II's Golden Jubilee, which was held in the grounds of Buckingham Palace. Dame Shirley also made an appearance in September at another Cinema Against AIDS event, as part of the International Venice Film Festival. She played a short set and was called back for an encore of 'I Am What I Am', from *La Cage Aux Folles*. The event raised over $500,000 for the AIDS charity amfAR. Another cinematic event came in December, when she took part in the BAFTA James Bond tribute, marking the fortieth anniversary of the character's first screen appearance.

*

In April 2003, the French government awarded Dame Shirley their highest honour, the Légion d'Honneur, which was presented to her in a private ceremony at the French Embassy in London. 'Now I'm a Dame and a Knight,' she quipped afterwards. That year she celebrated 50 years in show business with the album *Thank You For The Years*, and promoted it with six sell-out UK dates in June.

She also had a clearout of her wardrobe. Dame Shirley's old stage costumes had been stored in a London warehouse for years, and now she decided to part with 50 of them in a gala charity auction at the London auctioneers Christie's. As she explained, 'I would like to see them go while I'm alive . . . I want to see where they go and where the money goes. I don't want somebody fighting over them after I've gone. I've had great success from these gowns, and I'd like to see them go to a worthy cause.' She also stated her hopes that some of the dresses would end up in museums, and some in the collections of drag queens who'd impersonated her. Shirley herself bought one dress at the auction for £7,000 – the Welsh dragon flag dress, which she donated to the Royal Welsh College of Music and Drama.

'Dame Shirley Bassey: 50 Years Of Glittering Gowns' was held at Christie's on 18 September, and raised £250,000, which was divided equally between the two charities she had elected to support: the first being a Dame Shirley Bassey scholarship at the Royal Welsh College of Music and Drama, and the second the Noah's Ark Appeal, which was funding the building of a new children's hospital – the first ever to be built in Wales. Both charities were based in Cardiff, as Dame Shirley wanted 'to give something back to the city of my birth.'

Shirley's designer Douglas Darnell spent many hours meticulously arranging the gowns for display in the viewing room, but couldn't bear to stay for the auction and watch his work vanish forever. But Dame Shirley took an active hand in the auction proceedings, with bursts of impromptu singing from the auctioneer's rostrum, ending with 'The Party's Over.' Afterwards she joked, 'I have nothing to wear.'

Two further charity auctions would follow in 2005. When Dame Shirley sold her London apartment, many of its contents and furnishings were auctioned by the South London auctioneers Rosebery's, raising a further £25,000 for charity. There was a little embarrassment in store when it became known that some of the items auctioned had originally been presents from fans, and that some of Dame Shirley's awards (including some from the Variety Club) had also been mistakenly included. An apology was duly issued, and an attempt made to smooth any feathers that had been ruffled . . . but surely even divas are allowed to have a spring-clean once in a while?

Three months after the Rosebery's sale, Sotheby's auctioned off some antique furniture and paintings from Dame Shirley's Monaco apartment, apparently simply because she was trying to attain a more minimalist feel in her home; this time, £50,000 was raised.

*

In October 2003, Dame Shirley accepted a special award at the National Music Awards for Outstanding Contribution to Music; she then flew to New York, where she performed 'Goldfinger' at the Denise Rich Angel Ball, to raise money for cancer research. Returning to the UK in November, she accepted the *Western Mail*'s Lifetime Achievement award at their annual Welsh Woman of the Year awards. That year Dame Shirley had also seriously dated the theatrical producer Greg Smith, and was in a distinctly positive mood when interviewed at the Christie's auction: 'I've just recorded a fabulous album, I'm celebrating 50 years at the top, and I've met my man. I can't remember a moment when I looked forward with more hope.' Sadly, the relationship with Smith didn't last.

In January 2004, Dame Shirley was the headline performing act on the maiden voyage of the *Queen Mary 2* from Southampton to Florida. She'd sailed on the first *Queen Mary* back in the 1950s, and was looking forward to her trip on its replacement; unfortunately, one day out from shore the ship ran into a really severe storm, and Dame Shirley's performance had to be postponed by 24 hours owing to a bad bout of seasickness. The next day she rallied and gave two performances each in front of 1,000 passengers; at the first show she received eight standing ovations. Back in Britain that April, while attending the Chilled Pink charity benefit for childhood cancer, held at Quaglino's restaurant in South London, Dame Shirley won a pink Dyson vacuum cleaner in the prize draw. Quizzed by reporters as to whether she did her own housework, Dame Shirley replied, 'No, I don't, but I am going to start now.' So saying, she then rolled the Dyson over the carpet.

In September, Dame Shirley attended the Diamonds Are Forever Gala Ball at Cardiff's City Hall, another charity event in aid of the children's hospital Noah's Ark Appeal. Apart from raising money, the event was to acknowledge all Dame Shirley's fundraising work for the charity. The guests enjoyed a five-course gourmet dinner, while being entertained by the South Wales Male Voice Choir and mezzo-soprano Katherine Jenkins. After the dinner Dame Shirley auctioned off the white, crystal-encrusted gown that she was wearing (but refused requests to remove it on the spot), which raised another £7,000 for the appeal. The following day she toured the hospital, and visited the children's cancer outpatient unit that had been named after her.

*

During 2005 Dame Shirley made a lasting and important alliance when Catherine 'Been' Feeney and Nikki Lamborn, otherwise known as the London pop duo Never the Bride, entered her life. While spending a weekend in Monte Carlo, the duo had heard a rumour that their hotel was also the place where Dame Shirley was living. The receptionist informed them that although this rumour was untrue, Dame Shirley did in fact frequently use the hotel's gym. The girls left a copy of their CD *Surprise* with the receptionist, along with a note that read: 'Dear Dame Bassey, We think you would be fantastic doing track three, "The Living Tree".'

Several weeks later, Never the Bride received an e-mail from Dame Shirley informing them that she'd fallen head over heels in love with the song and was constantly playing it. She wanted to know who the writers were, and who owned the publishing rights. Several months later Been and Nikki met Dame Shirley in person at her hotel during one of her visits to London. The scheduled 20-minute meeting ended up lasting several hours, during which Dame Shirley announced that she intended to record 'The Living Tree' for her new album.

In September, Dame Shirley attended the unveiling ceremony when a paving stone featuring a star engraved with her name was set in the pavement outside St Paul's Church in Covent Garden, as part of London's 'Avenue of Stars' (she'd received a similar tribute in Rotterdam in 1991, in their Walk of Fame Starboulevard – and her name is also engraved on a paving stone in Cardiff's Bute Street, close to her birthplace). The following month she was one of 650 guests who attended a dinner to celebrate the eightieth birthday of Baroness Margaret Thatcher. That month Dame Shirley also recorded her second *Audience With Shirley Bassey* show for Granada TV, almost 10 years to the day after recording the first one. The show was broadcast the following March. In November, Dame Shirley took part once again in the Royal Variety Performance.

During 2006 several key figures seemed to vanish from Dame Shirley's immediate circle, including her manager John Webb, her publicist and Beaudoin Mills. She also expanded her presence on the Internet, with an official page on MySpace; announcements and messages both here and on her www.dameshirleybassey.com site were now frequently signed as originating from 'Camp DSB' (her current aides, presumably, including her PA Jenny Kern). That summer she played a series of gigs at large British arenas, ending Wembley Arena in June. She also appeared at the Bryn Terfel Faenol Festival in North Wales, and her performance there was subsequently broadcast by BBC Wales.

At the end of the year Dame Shirley appeared in a Christmas TV advertisement for Marks & Spencer, which featured all their contracted models (including Twiggy). The wintry-themed film was set in a glamorous ice palace hotel, exactly like the one that had featured in the James Bond movie *Die Another Day* – and the producers obviously felt that the ideal person to reinforce the ad's Bond motif was Dame Shirley Bassey, who appeared singing a cover version of Pink's anthemic dance number 'Get The Party Started' while wearing an M&S evening gown.

*

In March 2007 another auction of Dame Shirley's clothes and memorabilia took place at the Café de Paris. Titled 'Big Spenders', the auction – which was endorsed by Dame Shirley, although she was unable to attend personally – raised money for the children's charity Barnardo's. In April 'The Living Tree' was released as a single, having been produced by Never the Bride themselves. An epic, end-of-relationship statement of defiance, the single marked Dame Shirley's fiftieth anniversary in the British charts, entering at number 37.

Never the Bride had also produced 'Get the Party Started', the follow-up single, which was released on their own Lock Stock & Barrel label at the end of June (and signed for the rest of the world by Decca Records a few months later). The *Get The Party Started* album contained 'The Living Tree' as well as the title track, the remainder consisting of more remixes designed to appeal to club DJs, created by NorthxNWest, Cagedbaby, Ray Mang, Gilmmers, Knut Saevik and Paul 'Strangefruit' Nyhus, Bugz in the Attic, Phil Asher, the Left Side Of Dobie's Brain, Mark de Clive-Lowe and Bruno E. This time the results were far more of a mish-mash, and even the best of them was only mildly interesting; once again, in the main the original versions are preferable. The critics also found the album a very mixed bag. 'Some of it works, some of it clanks,' observed *Q* magazine's Peter Kane, while conceding that 'the lady herself remains a formidable force of nature.' *The Word*'s David Quantick pointed out that 'if it had come out in 1982 and been produced by B.E.F. or Neil Tennant, we'd all be calling it ironic genius.' Though the results were indeed mixed, the few moments when it really worked (the two Never the Bride tracks, and Bugz in the Attic's Latin treatment of 'What Now My Love') made one hope for more in the same vein to follow. The album entered the UK charts at number six (probably because the single was so good), and was dedicated to the memory of Samantha.

Dame Shirley spent most of that month in Britain promoting

the record on radio shows, as well as presenting an award at the British Soap Awards, for which she wore a new Vivienne Westwood gown. Been and Nikki had persuaded her that the new album should receive at least some live promotion as well, and to everyone's surprise Dame Shirley agreed to play at the Glastonbury Festival, her billing there promptly organized by promoter Harvey Goldsmith. (For an account of Dame Shirley's Glastonbury performance, see Introduction, p.1.) Dame Shirley publicly acknowledged her debt to Never the Bride by introducing them on stage during her Glastonbury set (although the *Guardian* reviewer rather unkindly dismissed them as 'two tattooed lesbians'). A few days later Dame Shirley attended Elton John's White Tie and Tiara Ball, which raised money for Elton's AIDS Foundation charity; the two duetted on a version of 'Big Spender' backed by a 25-piece orchestra, while the crowd of 500 celebrity invitees sang along for all they were worth.

*

Having teased the Arctic Monkeys from the Glastonbury stage, a few months later Dame Shirley was invited by *Q* magazine to present the band with their award for 'Best Act in the World Today.' Being a good sport, she obliged, and in September she happily rubbed shoulders and posed for photographs with all the rock musicians present at the *Q* Awards ceremony in London (while bemoaning the fact that there had been 'rather too much of the F-word for my liking' in the acceptance speeches); she also couldn't resist teasing Sir Paul McCartney ('You've always had a great butt! Let's have another look at it'), though he happily lifted up his jacket to oblige her. The only thing that marred this trip to London was the fact that a purse containing cash and credit cards was skilfully removed from Dame Shirley's handbag by a pickpocket while she was out shopping with her daughter in Knightsbridge. 'I can walk safely in Monte Carlo but not in London,' she observed sadly. Modern Britain, she feared, was 'not the country I remember growing up in.' She was also scathing about modern celebrity culture ('it seems that people want to be famous for doing nothing – or drinking'), and the fact that young singers all seemed to want short-cuts to success, and were no longer interested in actually learning their craft.

A few weeks later Dame Shirley presented another award, this time at the Pride of Britain Awards; she also briefly performed at the Albert Hall as part of the Fashion Rocks charity event. She ended the year with another single release which contained two remixes of 'Big Spender': one by NorthxNWest from the last album, and a new 'Pink Pound' mix (proving once again that she both had a sense of humour *and* knew who some of her fans were).

In December a belated seventieth birthday party was thrown for Dame Shirley by Andrew Davis, owner of Cliveden in Berkshire, and organized by her friend Liz Brewer. Cliveden is now an expensive hotel, but had once been a stately home belonging to the Astor family; the house had figured prominently in the Profumo affair, when Christine Keeler had cavorted naked in its swimming pool, and a few years later the Beatles had filmed a scene for *Help!* there. Party guests included Joan Collins, Cilla Black, Bruce Forsyth and Christopher Biggins; within days, an amusing clip surfaced on

YouTube of the birthday girl singing 'Happy Birthday to me' at the party, in the style of Marilyn Monroe.

Dame Shirley spent a quiet family Christmas with Sharon and her grandchildren at their home near Reading. She probably needed the rest; after all, it had been quite a year.

fifteen

THE LIFE

Although she still has a British passport – and also still pays British income tax whenever she works in England – ever since the early 1990s, Dame Shirley Bassey has lived for most of the year in Monte Carlo, in the principality of Monaco. She lives alone in an apartment overlooking the sea, and has many friends in the town; her neighbours include Ringo Starr and Boris Becker. 'The nicest thing about Monaco is that nobody bothers you at all,' she once said, and she has also claimed that she can sit on the beach all day and yet remain totally undisturbed by strangers, and wear jewellery in public with no fear of being robbed. This must bring a real sense of security, given that she once stated that she didn't want to hire a bodyguard because it would 'take all the enjoyment out of life.'

The décor in her apartment is a mixture of modern and antique ('furniture that I can look at and not get bored with'), with a number of European and African paintings ('I'm a big fan of art deco'), and her favourite room is her bedroom: 'It's huge, with a huge mirror and a huge television and a huge bed that would sleep about four.' There are also framed photographs on display, of both her daughters, of her four grandsons, Luke, Sebastian, Nathan and

Brett (now approximately aged between 13 and 28), and also of her adopted son Mark and his daughter Tatjana. In recent years Dame Shirley has described her daughter Sharon as 'my best friend'; Sharon has recently separated from her husband, and she and her mother talk frequently on the phone (though Dame Shirley has also joked acidly that this is because she's the one who foots the phone bill) and meet whenever Dame Shirley is in the UK. Both parties found it amusingly close to the truth when a journalist recently suggested that their mother-daughter relationship echoed that of Saffy and Edina in the sitcom *Absolutely Fabulous*. Sharon has repeatedly refused to speak to the press about her mother, although she did recently comment to a reporter from the *Daily Mail*, 'I will say that I am very proud of her.'

Sadly, Dame Shirley and Mark – who she once described as a 'naughty boy' – fell out badly after he sold his story to a tabloid newspaper. In it he had accused his mother of having drunken rows and affairs, and also admitted to his own history of cocaine and Ecstasy abuse. Mark lives in Marbella in Spain, and although he once received a generous monthly allowance from his mother, he is now apparently totally estranged from her.

There is also currently no man in Dame Shirley's life, something which she says 'suits me fine.' In the past she's been involved with both older men ('because I wanted a father figure') and younger men ('I wouldn't recommend it, because they haven't grown up, and they very quickly become rather boring and uninteresting. They just look good'); neither kind of relationship has worked for her in the long term. Once, despite being disillusioned, she still held out hope that she would find her dream man some day: 'I know from experience that it is not possible to combine family life with show business. If you are successful in my profession, there's no way you'll succeed in any other area. Nevertheless, I hope my fairy-tale will still have a happy ending, and that I have yet to find the True Love I have sung about for so long.' In more recent years she's described herself as being 'very comfortable in my own company. I don't mind not having a man in my life. It means that I can please myself and do the things that I want. I'm very happy going to bed on my own at 8 p.m., making a nest out of a great pile of pillows, watching TV and playing backgammon.' It's undoubtedly true that the demands of her professional life inevitably require a great deal of solitude. 'It is lonely, but sometimes you have to be lonely in order to do what you're doing,' she told the journalist and author Mona Bauwens for Bauwens' 1998 book *Feminine Power*. 'When I'm on a tour, I don't want anybody else around me. I wrap myself up in cotton-wool. I go from the hotel to the theatre and from the theatre on to the bus to the next town and the next hotel. It's complete dedication and it has to be that way. It's 100 per cent – you could give a little less, but I like to give 100 per cent, if not 110, and to do that I have to be on my own and be focused.' Yet she also obviously enjoys travelling on a tour bus, and once admitted that 'I really like to live out of a suitcase.'

Her lack of a romantic partner is something she ascribes at least partly to her own success: 'I came from a poor background and I made it in a man's world, but it was terribly difficult. I started off as a very cheerful, young, bright thing and I ended up as a hard, cold businesswoman in a man's world, which success brings. The business side makes you rather tough.' On another occasion she observed that, 'Men are afraid of powerful women,' pointing out that even the strong, confident men she has known have seemed jealous of the attention she receives in public. It was a matter she clarified further in 1998: 'Does an empowered woman need a powerful man? No, not at all. She's strong, but she needs a man to love and understand her and know what she's all about. Yes, I'd like to have a man in my life. It's nice to share. It's nice to go on a cruise with somebody you're romantically involved with. I've yet to meet the greatest love in my life. The men I'm attracted to don't have to be good-looking, but they have to have that animal sex appeal, and they have to have a sense of humour and not put me down because of who I am. It's unconditional love and wanting to be with me and I don't think that man exists. I've had most of the men I wanted, but I've not had the man I *really* want. Men and women are very, very different and we'll never understand each other, so I don't know why God made us for each other, maybe just to have babies because we really don't get along on a one-to-one basis.

'Men are comfortable with me because I make them feel comfortable, but in the long run it doesn't work. I'm a late-night person. I work late and even if I'm not working late I like to go out and I like to party and I'm out late. Even when I get home I cannot go to bed and I have to put on television and come down. I have to think about the evening and get things out of my system and if I'm with a man I can't do that. He doesn't want the television on, he wants to sleep right away and he's up early in the morning and I'm still asleep. So, it doesn't really work for me and it's better that I stay on my own. If I can have the occasional fling, then that's all right.'

Certainly it seems unlikely that she'll ever abandon her nocturnal lifestyle. She's lived this way for over 50 years, and it's unlikely she'll ever change. 'My body clock's *appalling*. It keeps me up. I don't get to sleep until four or five and even if I'm on vacation it doesn't change. I watch films for hours – thank God for Sky TV.'

Even when Dame Shirley isn't working, her daily routine doesn't vary that much. 'I never do lunch. I can't. I'm still getting out of bed.' On the rare occasions when she does go out in daylight, she usually wears a hat and sunglasses, and is seldom recognized unless she speaks, at which point her distinctive accent – a blend of transatlantic twang and Welsh lilt – betrays her: 'I'm disguised until I open my mouth. That's always a dead giveaway.' The purpose of these outings is usually for shopping, and she once confessed that she had 'a black belt in spending! I spend too much on clothes, which gives me a guilt complex because they don't get used. I never wear them. I go out and buy clothes on impulse, if I'm down to bring me up. It's like an aphrodisiac. I can easily spend £10,000 - £12,000 in one go. I like Sonia Rykiel, Tomasz Starzewski and I have quite a few Isabell Kristensen gowns. I like buying dresses, shoes, everything. I suppose I do it because I was the youngest of seven and as a child, I was dressed in hand-me-downs.' Her other great shopping weakness is for jewellery, and she's been known to buy 'a lot' via Sotheby's auctions all over the world.

She once owned villas in Sardinia and in Lugano in Switzerland, but these have long since been sold off. When she lived in those houses she always had a staff of several household servants, but in the end she found that the disadvantages of being an employer outweighed the comfort factor: 'You end up taking care of them.

They bring you their troubles. After that I said I never want to have any live-in servants again, so I have dailies that come in now and they go home when their work is finished, and I'm on my own.' These days she has a housekeeper, and is also assisted by a small secretarial staff.

She rises late in the day ('by the time I get the sleep out of my eyes, it's usually after two o'clock') and immediately splashes hot water on her face to wake herself up, after which she'll have a hot bath or shower, followed by a cold shower. Breakfast consists of black coffee and fresh fruit juice (a juicer always accompanies her on her travels, and she usually has vegetable juice in the evening). A couple of hours later she'll eat a couple of rice cakes with rose petal jam or mashed banana. If it's a day when she's working (rehearsing or performing), she'll head for the gym in the Grand Hotel, where she usually spends at least an hour; if she isn't working, she'll slob out in 'a long T-shirt and a tracksuit', and spend the afternoon reading, watching TV – tennis and cookery programmes are among her favourites – and talking on the phone. She'll then head for the gym about seven, where she'll stay for two hours before going out to dinner.

She once described her daily exercise regime: 'I stretch for half an hour, then I sit in a yoga position to do neck exercises and roll my head.' Rather than tiring her, she finds the process energizing, enough 'not only to throw my voice to the back of the auditorium, but also to be on stage as long as I am. I'm doing longer now than ever before – and with no pain at all at the end of it.' Several times a week she will also train in the gym with weights.

If it's a period when she's not performing, she often wakes up 'feeling terribly vulnerable for some reason. Maybe I've had a dream or I've been worrying about something before going to bed. The best thing to bring me back on track is to go to the gym and work out. Then I'm focused once again, and I can handle it.' The reason she can still wear strapless gowns on stage is because of her amazing skin tone, which she attributes to yoga, something she discovered in her youth. As to those gowns, they are mainly still designed by Douglas Darnell, or by Sarah Perceval. The initial ideas for the gowns are always hers, and she approves the designers' final drawings before they begin work.

If she's performing that night, the afternoon will be given over to rehearsal. Afterwards, she completely isolates herself in her dressing room, and only close associates are allowed to interrupt her solitude. She still suffers from nerves before each performance – the more so if a rehearsal has gone badly – and so she avoids any situation in which she may have to raise her voice, in order to avoid the risk of losing it. On stage, she's able to translate her occasional nervousness into physical movement, so the audience often remains unaware that she's a little jumpy.

She devotes the time before a show to doing her own make-up and generally trying to unwind. 'I don't do any exercises. It's basically a time for relaxing, and I just go into myself. And as I'm making up, I'm thinking of the songs that I'm going to sing. Of course, if one of the songs went badly in rehearsal then that's on my mind, and I keep going over that song to make sure that I stay focused on it, to avoid making the same mistake. Really, the whole preparation time is a time for focusing, for concentrating on what I'm about to do when I walk out onto that stage.' Although she'll sip champagne after a show, she now avoids all alcoholic drink beforehand. 'I might have a coffee, and I'll sip a lot of cold water, especially when I'm nervous, because it helps, just sipping. I'll occasionally break out into my vocals, just to make sure my voice is still there.'

Early on in her career she learned the hard way that thinking about her personal life while on stage could affect her performance adversely, and ever since she's tried to avoid doing so. Although the songs she sings 'do represent chunks of my life, of my own personal history', for her they belong to the past, not the present. 'I can't take the present on stage. I sing certain songs in a particular way because I've experienced what I'm singing about. If I were to take on stage with me something that was bothering me at present, I wouldn't be able to concentrate, to focus.'

After a show she may socialize with the fans that she frequently invites backstage, and she's been known to devote as much time and attention to old age pensioners as to celebrity friends. When they've all gone home, she's less likely to go nightclubbing than she once did, because she's no longer the wee-small-hours party girl she once was. 'To come as far as I have is a matter of having tremendous discipline, which I never had at one time. I'd party, and go to nightclubs until two or three in the morning. Then I'd go and do shows. But I realized as I got older that I couldn't do those things and two shows a night.' Instead, she tends to prefer quiet nights at home alone or with friends to the Monte Carlo highlife. 'I like to have friends over and I enjoy cooking for them. I like to cook, even if it's for just myself. I like to cook spaghetti, mushroom or vegetable risotto and I also love chicken and salmon. But I eat to live, not live to eat like some people. My tastes are quite simple. I love nothing more than a plate of chips and a bowl of ketchup to dip them in.'

Her health is largely good, perhaps because she pays so much attention to her diet and her exercise regime – although she no longer uses HRT, for very good reasons: five years of the treatment caused her oestrogen level to rise dangerously; additionally, she came close to developing diabetes, and if she'd carried on with HRT she would also have run a high risk of developing cancer. These days Dame Shirley avoids things she finds hard to digest (notably red meat), and takes multivitamins, rosehip, cod liver oil and herbal tea. She also fasts one day a week, taking only juice, water and herbal tea.

Is she happy? Content might be a better word. She once reminisced that her happiest time 'was when I was first started, because it was all great fun. I wasn't known, it was thrust upon me and I went along with it and I said, "I've got to do the best I can." At the beginning I loved it and I still do to a certain extent, but it's harder because success makes things hard, because life is never the same again. Now you're on top of the world everybody adores you. You're a big success, thousands of people come to see you and you're making *lots* of money, so things can never be like they were in the beginning. Now more concentration goes into it, you have to think more than ever what you're doing. It all becomes work, serious work, at which you can't fail, whereas when you're starting out you have nothing to lose and everything to gain.' Her work is the central part of her life and when she's not got a performance coming up she is often prone to what she calls a 'natural down', particularly in the early evening when she realizes that she's not going to be going on stage in a few hours' time.

In 1997 she claimed there had never been any big game plan for her career – it had just happened: 'I became my image. It's all really been out of my control. I've just gone along with it. Michael Sullivan started it and it's still going.'

*

The tabloid press have occasionally accused Dame Shirley of playing the diva, of acting high-handedly with staff and assistants, of throwing tantrums. Yet there are many who've worked with her who would rally to her defence, like hairdresser Derek Morris, who did Dame Shirley's hair for a Sainsbury's TV commercial: 'There was so much bad publicity about her at that time and, knowing that I was working with her the next day, I was filled with trepidation, but she couldn't have been nicer or funnier. She said, 'Do exactly what you want to do. I don't mind.' She trusted a complete stranger and I was very impressed with her. She's a very bright lady, warm and friendly. Her humour and my humour were on the same wavelength – we're both piss-takers, if you like. Nobody's at their best first thing in the morning, but she was the complete professional.'

Of course, the press doesn't want to hear that Dame Shirley is 'warm and friendly', because it doesn't make for a good story, or fit the image of her that they are trying to sell. So they persist in portraying her as 'difficult', which she naturally finds very hurtful: 'The woman is vulnerable and, even on stage, the vulnerability is there. Yet everybody says, "She must be very difficult to work with.

All those tantrums." There *are* no tantrums. I haven't got time for tantrums, and I would like that character to come over rather than the one that people hear about. Everybody wants to hear that stars are difficult. They prefer to hear that, but I've heard it long enough and it's about time somebody said, "She's vulnerable." There has to be vulnerability. It has to be there or I would not be making that contact with an audience. Of course it hurts when the press exaggerate my private life or they take words out of context. I don't know why they do it.'

Yet she also knows that the press can serve a positive purpose, albeit a sometimes painful one: 'I had a manager who said, "Don't only read the good notices, read the bad ones as well and learn." And he was right. Some that were really bad I kept and framed.'

*

'When I walk on stage I can tell immediately if I've got the audience,' Dame Shirley once stated – and yet when did she last encounter an audience that she didn't hold in the palm of her hand from the very first minute? After all, Dame Shirley's fans know exactly what they're going to get at one of her concerts, and – apart from the few occasions when she's had vocal problems – she has never failed to deliver the goods. Why does she continue to do it? Because, for her, it's addictive. She's even been able to go on stage while experiencing real physical pain, because 'the adrenalin acts like a painkiller and it goes away while you're on stage.'

Discussing her 1997 Birthday Concert at Althorp Park, Simon Fanshawe wrote in the *Sunday Times* that her audience consisted of:

the burghers of Middle England gathered to celebrate their idol and her mastery of the stylishly vulgar. With their M&S picnics and their hampers, and some of them even in dinner jackets, it was a middle-market Glyndebourne without the opera, but most definitely with a star. Her stagecraft is supreme. As she stood swathed in sparkling white, the feathers on the hood of her cloak fluttering in the wind around the soft brown of her face, you realized that she has made an entire career out of entrances and exits. The crowd literally worships her. They hold out gifts of flowers, champagne and soft toys.

'They overwhelm me,' she says in the ordinary light of day. 'I feel like I am,' she pauses '. . . some goddess, and they are giving up an offering. Sometimes I go home to my hotel room after the show and these thoughts come to me. Why do they do this? Why do they reach out to me like that? Why do they give me these gifts?' She seems to have no answers herself. It may seem a little silly to put it like this, but they do it because she is 'Shirley Bassey.' She is the creation of a life lived in public. She is their creation and, even on stage with an orchestra and in front of thousands, she is truly alone.

Goddesses derive splendour from their isolation. Her audience is in awe but also perhaps they are offering gifts of consolation as a hedge against their own solitude. What they get in return is her total commitment. 'Their applause is thrilling, incredible. And, of course, I need it. It's what keeps me going. It's my life.'

It's as good a summing up as any, and there remains very little to add. In recent years Dame Shirley has spent as much as seven months of the year touring the world, and her charity performances are far more numerous than the ones I've listed in this book; small wonder that she's often spoken of a time when she'll be free from her career and able to 'go explore the Pyramids and all the places I've wanted to visit but haven't had the time to. I'm a gypsy, you see. I love a good adventure.' But every time she seriously considers retiring – or even slowing down – yet more offers of work flood in from all over the world, and she takes to the road once again. Since the power of her voice is undiminished, and most of its vocal range remains intact, it seems very unlikely that Dame Shirley Bassey will ever stop performing in concert, as long as her health permits and there are audiences who want to see her; if she has her own way, she'll probably choose to die with those diamanté-studded boots on.

sixteen

THE FUTURE

In January 2008, Dame Shirley celebrated her seventy-first birthday in Los Angeles; then she was off on the road again, this time to promote her *Get The Party Started* album around the world. 2007 had raised her public profile higher than it had been for years, but could she now find a way to sustain that level of interest?

For despite her undoubted financial success, her loyal fan following and the fact that all her concert dates sell out almost immediately, it would not be inaccurate to say that Dame Shirley Bassey has been somewhat creatively undervalued to date. For example, she has yet to receive the kind of comprehensive CD retrospective treatment that one would expect as the due for an artist of her stature and vintage (ideally, something like a 4-CD boxed set that covered her entire career), and her early recordings on the Philips label have never been issued on CD at all.

At the end of 2007 some of those earliest recordings came out of copyright, and as a result, in January 2008 Stage Door Records issued *Shirley Bassey: The Early Years*, which comprised 19 tracks recorded during 1956 and 1957 (five of them recorded live at the Café de Paris). The sound quality isn't wonderful, since the CD had been sourced from old vinyl records, but the material itself is fascinating. On the studio recordings (which include 'Burn My Candle' and 'The Banana Boat Song') the young Shirley sounds sultrier than one might expect, but she has obviously yet to gain complete control of her voice and has not yet found her own vocal style – there are echoes of Billie Holiday and Ella Fitzgerald, and what would later become the Bassey voice we all know is only hinted at here. Most of the material has a swing feel to it, though the worst tracks are little more than novelty numbers ('tra la la, you're as sweet as a candy bar') and even the good songs are often marred by the irritating background vocals which were practically a trademark of the era. That said, a good half-dozen of the studio tracks are well worth hearing, and the five live tracks are much better; a year further on into her professional career, young Shirley sounds far more relaxed and assured, and the simpler musical setting provided by the club's band only works to her advantage. In the light of these recordings, one can only hope that Dame Shirley does finally get around to recording a whole new album of blues and classic R&B material (which is definitely not to be confused with the modern variety of R&B, which tends to be bland in the extreme), as she has been promising for years. If one might make a suggestion, Jools Holland (for one) would probably be delighted to produce such a work.

As to Dame Shirley's own desires for the future, they probably aren't much different from the ones she outlined in 1998: 'I just want to carry on singing and finding unusual songs, songs that challenge. Wearing those glamorous gowns, making people happy, seeing people stand up – which is the greatest thing in the world.

It's better than sex, because it lasts so long after I've come off stage, and it can even last until the next day. It gets me on such a high. It's what every singer, every entertainer, dreams about. A standing ovation. It's a tremendous feeling, because it means you've pulled it off, you've done the job so well that these people are standing and telling you so.'

Which takes us back to Glastonbury, in a sense. Dame Shirley was by no means the first 'old school' star to find favour with the Glastonbury crowd. In 1994 Johnny Cash was also given a standing ovation there, which moved him to tears – and the crowd was cheering him not only because of his old material, but because of his current work as well. In his twilight years Cash found in Rick Rubin the most sympathetic and supportive record producer he'd ever had, who not only encouraged him to record songs he'd loved all his life, but also brought him new ones to cover. Getting Cash to sing material by modern songwriters (most notably his recording of Trent Reznor's 'Hurt') was not only a critical masterstroke, but a commercial one as well, since it brought the singer to the attention of a much younger audience than the one he'd been used to reaching. It was perhaps the same logic that led Never the Bride to suggest that Dame Shirley should cover a Pink song, with undeniably effective results. Through her work with artists like Yello, the Propellerheads and Never the Bride, Dame Shirley seems, like Cash, to have been adopted by a generation of younger artists eager to work with her.

There are certainly a good many other modern and 'unusual songs' out there that she could also embrace – one which immediately leaps to mind is Amy Winehouse's 'Back To Black', which sounds as if it could have been written specifically with Dame Shirley in mind . . . and Dame Shirley herself is known to like Winehouse's work. In the summer of 2007 she publicly supported producer David Arnold's stated desire that Amy Winehouse should sing the theme for the next James Bond movie (the twenty-second): 'There aren't many female artists of her generation with such an unusual sound. I can't think of anybody better to sing the Bond theme tune.'

But the late twentieth century was positively crowded with good songwriters. Dame Shirley has been known to cover Madonna and Grace Jones songs in concert, so why shouldn't she check out Prince's back catalogue as well? The possibilities are almost endless, if she can only find the right producer – hopefully one as simpatico as Rick Rubin was for Johnny Cash. Possibly Never the Bride could fulfil that role for her, but their future collaborative plans are unknown (and, unfortunately, they also declined to be interviewed for this book). All that is known through Dame Shirley's official website is the fact that 'some major artists' are said to be interested in collaborating with her. One of these may well be Pink, who was apparently so pleased with Dame Shirley's cover of 'Get The Party Started' that in August 2007 she suggested that she should perform a duet with the Dame: 'She has a great voice, and I have a fantastic idea of a song for us.'

Whatever comes next, it can only make an interesting addition to what has already been a quite extraordinary life – and a quite unique talent.

Index